CLEAN JOKES
forKids

BARBOUR
PUBLISHING, INC.
Uhrichsville, Ohio

Published byBarbour Publishing, Inc.
        P.O. Box 719
        Uhrichsville, Ohio 44683
        http://www.barbourbooks.com

 Member of the
Evangelical Christian
Publishers Association

Printed in the United States of America.

ANIMALS

What do you call a puppy who loves anchovies and garlic?
A dog whose bark is a thousand times worse than his bite.

∧∧∧∧∧∧∧∧∧∧∧∧∧∧∧∧∧∧∧∧∧∧∧∧∧∧∧∧

Why do skunks smell so bad?
Cheap cologne.

∧∧∧∧∧∧∧∧∧∧∧∧∧∧∧∧∧∧∧∧∧∧∧∧∧∧∧∧

Why did the cow enroll in drama class?
To become a moo-vie star.

3

Where do space explorers leave their space-craft?
At parking meteors.

∧∧∧∧∧∧∧∧∧∧∧∧∧∧∧∧∧∧∧∧∧∧∧∧∧∧∧∧∧∧

Why did the dog lie on its back with its feet sticking straight into the air?
It hoped to trip the birds.

∧∧∧∧∧∧∧∧∧∧∧∧∧∧∧∧∧∧∧∧∧∧∧∧∧∧∧∧∧∧

What's minty, pasty, dangerous, and kills germs?
Shark-infested toothpaste.

∧∧∧∧∧∧∧∧∧∧∧∧∧∧∧∧∧∧∧∧∧∧∧∧∧∧∧∧∧∧

Why did the zoo veterinarian refuse to wear a necktie?
She already had a boa-tie.

Lorraine: "Did you know that your dog and
    my dog are brother and sister?"
Larry: "Great! That means we're related!"

∧∧∧∧∧∧∧∧∧∧∧∧∧∧∧∧∧∧∧∧∧∧∧∧∧∧∧

Why does a bear hibernate for three months
    in cold weather?
We're all afraid to wake it up!

∧∧∧∧∧∧∧∧∧∧∧∧∧∧∧∧∧∧∧∧∧∧∧∧∧∧∧

What kind of animal
    always is found at
    baseball games?
The bat.

∧∧∧∧∧∧∧∧∧∧

"Tracie's dog looks just
    like a member of her
    family," said Stacie.
"Which one?" asked
    Macie.

What keys are found in the animal kingdom?
Donkeys, monkeys and turkeys.

∧∧∧∧∧∧∧∧∧∧∧∧∧∧∧∧∧∧∧∧∧∧∧∧∧∧∧∧

How do you snatch a rug from under a polar bear?
Wait 'til the bear migrates.

∧∧∧∧∧∧∧∧∧∧∧∧∧∧∧∧∧∧∧∧∧∧∧∧∧∧∧∧

What's a lamb's favorite department store?
Woolworth's.

∧∧∧∧∧∧∧∧∧∧∧∧∧∧∧∧∧∧∧∧∧∧∧∧∧∧∧∧

What did Natasha do when she found her pet dog eating her dictionary?
She took the words right out of his mouth.

Ingrid had caught a pond turtle and kept it in captivity for a couple of days, until her parents convinced her the little animal would be much happier in the wild. Her mother was very pleased when she saw Ingrid carrying the turtle out the back door.

"Where are you taking it?" her mother asked.

"Back to the pond."

"That's wonderful, Honey!"

But the next day, Ingrid's mother noticed the turtle was still around. She saw Ingrid walking out the front door with it in her palm.

"I thought you let the turtle free yesterday," her mother said.

"No, I just took it back to the pond for a visit. Today I'm taking it to the beach."

Why do moose have fur coats?
They don't like wearing cotton.

∧∧∧∧∧∧∧∧∧∧∧∧∧∧∧∧∧∧∧∧∧∧∧∧∧∧∧∧∧∧∧

Mike: "I heard you got kicked out of the zoo
  last week."
Ike: "Yeah, for feeding the squirrels."
Mike: "Wow, I know they don't like for people to feed the animals, but that seems
  like strong punishment."
Ike: "Actually, I was feeding the squirrels to
  the cougars."

∧∧∧∧∧∧∧∧∧∧∧∧∧∧∧∧∧∧∧∧∧∧∧∧∧∧∧∧∧∧∧

"Did you know Bobby's in the hospital?"
  Tracie asked.
"No, what happened?" Laurie replied.
"He went to the zoo, and the zookeeper told
  him the alligator would eat off his hand.
  So he gave it a try."

Malcolm: "Dad, when you cut down a tree, isn't it true that a new tree sometimes grows out of the stump?"

Dad: "Yes, that's been known to happen."

Malcolm: "Then if you cut off my pony's tail, will a new pony grow out of the tail?"

^^^^^^^^^^^^^^^^^^^^^^^^^^^^^^^^^^

What's black and white and furry and moves on 16 wheels?
A skunk on skates.

^^^^^^^^^^^^^^^^^^^^^^^^^^^^^^^^^^

How do you make a skunk stop smelling?
Cut off its nose.

Martha: "I hear you've been cruel to your cat."

Jeremy: "Nonsense. I simply twirl its tail around in the air occasionally."

∧∧∧∧∧∧∧∧∧∧∧∧∧∧∧∧∧∧∧∧∧∧∧∧∧∧∧∧

Lindsay: "Has is ever occurred to you that humans are the only animals who smoke cigarettes?"

Todd: "Well, we're the only animals who know how to strike matches."

∧∧∧∧∧∧∧∧∧∧∧∧∧∧∧∧∧∧∧∧∧∧∧∧∧∧∧∧

Where's the best place to park dogs?
In a barking lot.

∧∧∧∧∧∧∧∧∧∧∧∧∧∧∧∧∧∧∧∧∧∧∧∧∧∧∧∧

Why did the mouse give up tap dancing?
It kept falling in the sink.

Maria: "I can always tell when my dog is happy."

Michael: "Does he wag his tail?"

Maria: "No, but he stops biting me."

^^^^^^^^^^^^^^^^^^^^^^^^^^^^

Blake: "My dog's the smartest in town. He can say his own name in perfect English."

Alice: "What's his name?"

Blake: "Ruff."

^^^^^^^^^^^

What do you get when you cross a polar bear and a sloth?

A giant, white, furry animal that sleeps while hanging upside-down from icicles.

11

Why do coyotes call at night?
The rates are cheaper.

∧∧∧∧∧∧∧∧∧∧∧∧∧∧∧∧∧∧∧∧∧∧∧∧∧∧∧∧∧

How do you catch a rabbit?
Hide in the bushes and sound like a carrot.

∧∧∧∧∧∧∧∧∧∧∧∧∧∧∧∧∧∧∧∧∧∧∧∧∧∧∧∧∧

Why did the goat stick its head through the
    barbed wire fence?
To see what was on the other side.

∧∧∧∧∧∧∧∧∧∧∧∧∧∧∧∧∧∧∧∧∧∧∧∧∧∧∧∧∧

Nina: "I heard you just got back from
    Africa! Did you hunt wild game?"
Stevie: "Yeah, lions."
Nina: "Did you have any luck?"
Stevie: "Yep. Didn't see a one."

What's grey and has four legs and a trunk?
a mouse on vacation.

^^^^^^^^^^^^^^^^^^^^^^^^^^^^^^^^^^

How do you save a hippopotamus drowning
   in hot cocoa?
Throw it a marshmallow.

^^^^^^^^^^^^^^^^^^^^^^^^^^^^^^

What kind of dog directs traffic?
a police dog.

^^^^^^^^^

How do you know
   if there's a
   bear in your
   toothpaste?
*The toothbrush is
   too heavy to lift.*

What do you call a flying ape?
A hot-air baboon.

^^^^^^^^^^^^^^^^^^^^^^^^^^^^^^^^

oinkment: medicine for a pig with sore
muscles.

^^^^^^^^^^^^^^^^^^^^^^^^^^^^^^^^

What do you do when a mouse squeaks?
Oil it.

^^^^^^^^^^^^^^^^^^^^^^^^^^^^^^^^

Why does the giraffe have a long neck?
So it won't have to smell its feet.

^^^^^^^^^^^^^^^^^^^^^^^^^^^^^^^^

Why can't you telephone the zoo?
The lion's busy.

A pet shop owner was trying to talk Mrs. McLellan into buying a dog for her children. "Oh, they'll love this little rascal!" said the clerk. "He's full of fun and he eats anything. He especially likes children."

^^^^^^^^^^^^

What's black and white and has a red nose?
Rudolph the red-nosed zebra.

^^^^^^^^^

What was the dog doing in the mud puddle?
Making mutt pies.

Tim: "I've heard bears won't chase you at night if you carry a flashlight."

Kim: "Depends on how fast you carry it."

∧∧∧∧∧∧∧∧∧∧∧∧∧∧∧∧∧∧∧∧∧∧∧∧∧∧∧∧∧

What do rats keep in the glove compartments of their cars?

Rodent maps.

∧∧∧∧∧∧∧∧∧∧∧∧∧∧∧∧∧∧∧∧∧∧∧∧∧∧∧∧∧

What was the turtle doing on the Los Angeles freeway?

Record time.

∧∧∧∧∧∧∧∧∧∧∧∧∧∧∧∧∧∧∧∧∧∧∧∧∧∧∧∧∧

Teacher: If I give you four hamsters and your brother three hamsters, how many hamsters will you have altogether?

Student: Ten. We have three already.

What's green and white and green and white and green and white?
An alligator somersaulting downhill.

∧∧∧∧∧∧∧∧∧∧∧∧∧∧∧∧∧∧∧∧∧∧∧∧∧∧∧∧∧∧

What's the favorite city of hamsters?
Hamsterdam.

∧∧∧∧∧∧∧∧∧∧

What's the favorite city of chickens?
Chicago.

∧∧∧∧∧∧∧

Where do sheep get their hair cut?
At the baa-ber shop.

Why did the cow jump over the moon?
It forgot where it left its rocket ship.

∧∧∧∧∧∧∧∧∧∧∧∧∧∧∧∧∧∧∧∧∧∧∧∧∧∧∧∧∧

What do you call a bull taking a nap?
A bulldozer.

∧∧∧∧∧∧∧∧∧∧∧∧∧∧∧∧∧∧∧∧∧∧∧∧∧∧∧∧∧

A flock of lambs were playing in the meadow. "Baa! Baa! Baa!" they called merrily—except one lamb who insisted, "Moo! Moo! Moo!"

"What are you saying?" they demanded.

"I'm practicing a foreign language."

∧∧∧∧∧∧∧∧∧∧∧∧∧∧∧∧∧∧∧∧∧∧∧∧∧∧∧∧∧

Where do sheep go on vacation?
To the Baahaamaas.

Where does the farmer wash his livestock?
At the hogwash.

^^^^^^^^^^^^^^^^^^^^^^^^^^^^^^^^

How do you count a herd of cows?
With a cowculator.

^^^^^^^^^^^

Where do cows
   go on dates?
To the moovies.

^^^^^^^^^^^

Sue: "Dogs are ter-
   rible dancers."
Allen: "How do you
   know that?"
Sue: "They have two
   left feet."

What did Shane say when his pet snake
    crawled into the garbage disposal?
"It won't be long, now."

∧∧∧∧∧∧∧∧∧∧∧∧∧∧∧∧∧∧∧∧∧∧∧∧∧∧∧∧∧∧

Bart: "Our house was robbed last night
    while we were out."
Bret: "But I thought Butch was a great
    watchdog."
Bart: "Apparently he watched them take
    everything in sight."

∧∧∧∧∧∧∧∧∧∧∧∧∧∧∧∧∧∧∧∧∧∧∧∧∧∧∧∧∧∧

Why doesn't the cow wear a bell?
Two horns are enough warning.

∧∧∧∧∧∧∧∧∧∧∧∧∧∧∧∧∧∧∧∧∧∧∧∧∧∧∧∧∧∧

Where do injured rabbits go?
    To the hopspital.

Police were investigating a break-in.
"Didn't you hear any strange noises next
    door last evening?" they asked one
    neighbor.
"We couldn't hear anything. Their dog was
    barking too loud."

∧∧∧∧∧∧∧∧∧∧∧∧∧∧∧∧∧,

Why do firemen keep
    Dalmatians?
*To find the fire
    hydrants.*

∧∧∧∧∧,

What do you call
    a mild-mannered
    snake?
a civil serpent.

Where do all the jungle animals like to eat lunch?

At the beastro.

∧∧∧∧∧∧∧∧∧∧∧∧∧∧∧∧∧∧∧∧∧∧∧∧∧∧∧

Teacher: "Jerry, name an animal that's a carnivore."

Jerry: "A tiger."

Teacher: "That's good. Beryl, can you name a carnivore?"

Beryl: "Another tiger."

∧∧∧∧∧∧∧∧∧∧∧∧∧∧∧∧∧∧∧∧∧∧∧∧∧∧∧

Rachel: "Did you know dogs eat more than elephants?"

Penny: "No way! How can they do that?"

Rachel: "There are thousands of times more dogs in the world than there are elephants."

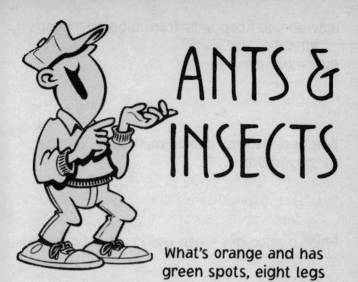

ANTS & INSECTS

What's orange and has green spots, eight legs and one red eye?
I give up. What?
I don't know, but there's one crawling up your back.

^^^^^^^^^^^^^^^^^^^^^^^^^^^^^^^^^^^

Why do spiders spin webs?
No one's ever taught them to crochet.

How do you keep ants from digging mounds all over your yard?
Take away their shovels.

∧∧∧∧∧∧∧∧∧∧∧∧∧∧∧∧∧∧∧∧∧∧∧∧∧∧∧∧∧∧

Where do worms prefer to shop?
In the Big Apple.

∧∧∧∧∧∧∧∧∧∧∧∧∧∧∧∧∧∧∧∧∧∧∧∧∧∧∧∧∧∧

What do you get when you cross a tiger and a gnat?
A man-eating gnat.

∧∧∧∧∧∧∧∧∧∧∧∧∧∧∧∧∧∧∧∧∧∧∧∧∧∧∧∧∧∧

Teacher: "The ant is a very industrious creature. It never seems to stop working —and do you see what it has to show for it?"
Student: "Yeah, it gets stepped on."

Two fleas hopped down the steps onto the sidewalk. One turned to the other and asked, "Should we walk, or take a dog?"

^^^^^^^^^^^^^^^^^^^^^^^^^^^^^^^^^^^^^

Jim and Ward were camping out one summer evening, and mosquitoes were a terrible problem. About dark, a different type of insect made its presence known: fireflies, darting here and there throughout the forest.

"Wow! Look at those mosquitoes!" cried Jim.

"Oh, no!" Ward said. "I thought we could hide from them in the dark, but they're coming after us with flash-lights!"

Why did the flea work overtime?
It was saving up to buy a dog.

∧∧∧∧∧∧∧∧∧∧∧∧∧∧∧∧∧∧∧∧∧∧∧∧∧∧∧∧∧

Why do hikers wear boots with ridged
  soles?
So ants will have an even chance.

∧∧∧∧∧∧∧∧∧∧∧∧∧∧∧∧∧∧∧∧∧∧∧∧∧∧∧∧

Nell: "Is it true that ants are the hardest-
  working creatures?"
Science Teacher: "That's what a lot of scien-
  tists believe."
Nell: "Then why are they always attending
  picnics?"

∧∧∧∧∧∧∧∧∧∧∧∧∧∧∧∧∧∧∧∧∧∧∧∧∧∧∧∧

Did the worms enter Noah's ark in pairs?
No, in apples.

AUTOMOBILES

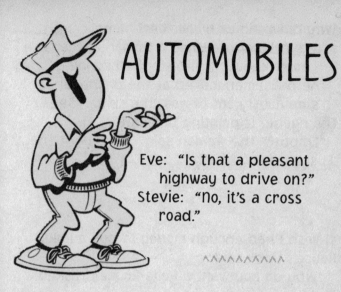

Eve: "Is that a pleasant highway to drive on?"
Stevie: "No, it's a cross road."

∧∧∧∧∧∧∧∧∧∧

Why can't car mufflers participate in marathon races?
They're too exhausted.

∧∧∧∧∧∧∧∧∧∧∧∧∧∧∧∧∧∧∧∧∧∧∧∧∧∧

Why did the tire get fired from its job?
It couldn't stand the pressure.

"What's wrong with your car?" a policeman asked as he approached a woman at roadside.

"I don't know. It just stopped running."

The policeman looked at the dashboard. "It's obviously out of gas," he said. "See? The needle is pointing to 'empty.' "

"Empty?" the woman said. "I thought the 'E' stood for 'enough.' "

^^^^^^^^^^^^^^^^^^^^^^^^^^^^^^^^^

"I wish I had enough money to buy a Rolls-Royce," Jory said.

"Why do you want a Rolls-Royce?" asked Floyd.

"I don't. It's the money I want."

^^^^^^^^^^^^^^^^^^^^^^^^^^^^^^^^^

Maria: "What would you do if you were being chased by a runaway tractor-trailer truck at 70 miles an hour?"

Karl: "Eighty."

Maggie and Sarah were driving to a party at a friend's house. The friend lived on a winding road off another winding road off another winding road in a very large neighborhood. Finally, they arrived.

"Well, I got us here," Maggie said, "but I may have to drive around awhile before I can find the right road home."

"Why can't you just put the car in reverse?" Sarah asked.

BABIES

Shirley: "I weighed only 2 pounds when I was born."

Ellen: "Wow! Did you survive?"

∧∧∧∧∧∧∧∧∧∧∧∧∧∧∧∧∧∧∧∧∧∧∧∧∧∧∧∧

Mother scolded her 2-year-old daughter, "Jacqueline, stop sucking your thumb."

"Why, Mommy?" little Jacqueline asked.

"It may be poisonous."

∧∧∧∧∧∧∧∧∧∧∧∧∧∧∧∧∧∧∧∧∧∧∧∧∧∧∧∧

Kendall: "Mommy, there's a woman at the
    door with a baby."
Mommy: "Well, tell her we don't need any-
    more."

∧∧∧∧∧∧∧∧∧∧∧∧∧∧∧∧∧∧∧∧∧∧∧∧∧∧∧∧

Liz: "We've found a way to keep my baby
    brother from spilling his food all over the
    table."
Melinda: "How?"
Liz: "We've started feeding
    him on the floor."

∧∧∧∧∧∧∧∧∧∧∧∧∧∧∧∧∧∧

"What's your baby brother's
    name?"
"Don't know. He won't tell
    anybody."

BIBLE JOKES

Alice: "Grandma, were you on Noah's ark?"

Grandma: "Oh, no."

Alice: "Then how did you survive the flood?"

^^^^^^^^^^^^^^^^^^^^^^^^^^^^^^^^^^

Who was the first tennis player in the Bible?
Joseph. He served in Pharoah's court.

Sunday school teacher: "Nora, what does the Bible have to say about the Dead Sea?"

Nora: "Dead? I didn't even know it was ill!"

^^^^^^^^^^^^^^^^^^^^^^^^^^^^^^^^^^^^

The Sunday School teacher asked her pupils to draw a picture of Joseph, Mary and the Christ child fleeing from Herod. Margie drew an airplane with three faces looking out the windows.

"That's interesting," the teacher said. "Where are they going?"

"Egypt," Margie replied.

"By airplane?"

"Yes, Pontius the pilot is driving."

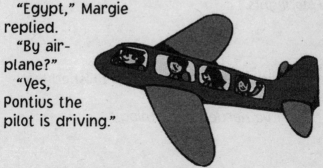

Shelby: "Do you know at what point in history God created Eve?"
Sandra: "Right after He created Adam."

∧∧∧∧∧∧∧∧∧∧∧∧∧∧∧∧∧∧∧∧∧∧∧∧∧∧∧∧

Who was most sorry when the Prodigal Son returned home?
The fatted calf.

∧∧∧∧∧∧∧∧∧∧∧∧∧∧∧∧∧∧∧∧∧∧∧∧∧∧∧∧

What kind of lights did Noah put on the ark?"
Floodlights.

∧∧∧∧∧∧∧∧∧∧∧∧∧∧∧∧∧∧∧∧∧∧∧∧∧∧∧∧

What did Noah say when he'd finished loading the ark?
"Now I've herded everything."

BIRDS & BEES

What did the parrot say
on Independence
Day?
Polly wanna firecracker.

ᐱᐱᐱᐱᐱᐱᐱᐱᐱᐱᐱᐱᐱᐱᐱᐱᐱᐱᐱᐱᐱᐱᐱᐱ

Why won't you find much honey grown in
Maryland?
There's only one "B" in Baltimore.

Brother: "It's a good thing you're not a swan."

Sister: "Why not?"

Brother: "You can't swim and you can't fly."

∧∧∧∧∧∧∧∧∧∧∧∧∧∧∧∧∧∧∧∧∧∧∧∧∧∧∧∧∧∧

Why do hummingbirds hum?
They've never learned the words.

∧∧∧∧∧∧∧∧∧∧∧∧∧∧∧∧∧∧∧∧∧∧∧∧∧∧∧∧∧∧

Farmer Brown and Farmer Jones were sitting in front of the country store listening to the birds in the distance.

"There's an old owl," said Farmer Brown. "Can you hear it call, 'Hoo, hoo?' "

"That's not an owl," said Farmer Jones. "It's a dove. It's saying, 'Coo, coo.' "

Farmer Brown shook his head sadly.

"I'm ashamed to say I know you. You don't recognize a 'hoo' from a 'coo.' "

36

What's the easiest way to imitate a bird?
Eat worms.

∧∧∧∧∧∧∧∧∧∧∧∧∧∧∧∧∧∧∧∧∧∧∧∧∧∧∧∧

What goes "quick-quick?"
A duck with the hiccups.

∧∧∧∧∧∧∧∧∧∧∧∧∧∧∧∧∧∧∧∧∧∧∧∧∧∧∧∧

Where do you treat an injured wasp?
At the waspital.

∧∧∧∧∧∧∧∧∧∧∧∧∧∧∧∧∧∧∧∧∧∧∧∧∧∧∧∧

Mickie: "My bulldog came away from the
    bird show with first prize."
Vickie: "How could
    a dog do
    that?"
Mickie: "He ate
    the winning
    parrot."

Sissy: "Have you heard they're now making a special kind of ground meat out of bumblebees?"

Missy: "Yuk! What do they call that?"

Sissy: "Humburger."

∧∧∧∧∧∧∧∧∧∧∧∧∧∧∧∧∧∧∧∧∧∧∧∧∧∧∧∧∧

How do you tell a male robin from a female robin?

Call it by name. If he answers, it's a male. If she answers, it's a female.

∧∧∧∧∧∧∧∧∧∧∧∧∧∧∧∧∧∧∧∧∧∧∧∧∧∧∧∧∧

Where on Noah's ark did the bees stay?

In the ark hives.

∧∧∧∧∧∧∧∧∧∧∧∧∧∧∧∧∧∧∧∧∧∧∧∧∧∧∧∧∧

Why do owls fly around at night?

It's faster than walking.

What do you call a duck's last will and testament?
a legal duckument.

^^^^^^^^^^^^^^^^^^^^^^^^^^^^^^^^^^^^^^

Where do ducks prefer to go on vacation?
The Duck-otas.

^^^^^^^^^^^^^^

Where do wasps live?
Stingapore.

^^^^^^^^^^

Why did Judy keep her pet bird in a fish bowl?
The water wouldn't stay in a cage.

What goes "peck-peck-peck-peck" and usually points to the north?
a magnetic woodpecker.

∧∧∧∧∧∧∧∧∧∧∧∧∧∧∧∧∧∧∧∧∧∧∧∧∧∧∧∧∧

A band of pirates buried their treasure on the seashore. Afterward, they looked around for a marker but could find nothing except a few ostrich eggs. So they broke open the eggs, fried the yolks and left the shells on top of the buried treasure.
The pirate captain announced to his crew, "Eggs mark the spot."

∧∧∧∧∧∧∧∧∧∧∧∧∧∧∧∧∧∧∧∧∧∧∧∧∧∧∧∧∧

What do you get when you cross a parrot with a whippoorwill?
a bird that can sing both the words and the music.

Candice: "I'm afraid to buy eggs at the supermarket, because when I break them open at home I might discover they have little chicks inside them."

Lennie: "Then why don't you buy goose eggs?"

^^^^^^^^^^^^^^^^^^^^^^^^^^^^^^

Bonnie: "Our parakeet bit my finger again this morning."

Benny: "Did you have to put anything on it?"

Bonnie: "Oh, no. He likes it plain."

^^^^^^^^

What do you call the Marines' pet bird?
a parrot trooper.

What do you say to a 200-pound parrot?
*"Here's your box of crackers. What else
   would you like?"*

∧∧∧∧∧∧∧∧∧∧∧∧∧∧∧∧∧∧∧∧∧∧∧∧∧∧∧∧∧

What kind of birds live in Central America?
Birds with suntans.

∧∧∧∧∧∧∧∧∧∧∧∧∧∧∧∧∧∧∧∧∧∧∧∧∧∧∧∧∧

How can you tell a guy hummingbird from a
   girl hummingbird?
By his mustache.

BOOKS

Little Lauren stomped up to the return desk at a department store. "Is it really true you'll give me a refund if I'm not fully satisfied with one of your products?" she asked the clerk.

"Certainly," said the clerk.

"Good," Lauren said, putting a new paperback novel on the counter. "I bought this here last week, and I don't like the ending."

Mitzy: "I just read a very stirring book."
Gordon: "What was it about?"
Mitzy: "Cooking."

^^^^^^^^^^^^^^^^^^^^^^^^^^^^^^^^^

A man in a bookstore wanted to buy a book titled *How to Become a Billionaire Overnight*. But some of the pages were missing, so he complained to the shop owner.

"What's the problem?" asked the owner. "You'll still become at least a millionaire."

CHICKEN JOKES

What parrot was a famous Antarctic explorer?

Admiral Bird.

^^^^^^^^^^^^^^^^^^^^^^^^^^^^^^^^

Who was the least favorite president of chickens?

Herbert Hoover. "A chicken in every pot," he promised.

What's the favorite sport of platypuses?
Bill-iards.

∧∧∧∧∧∧∧∧∧∧∧∧∧∧∧∧∧∧∧∧∧∧∧∧∧∧∧∧∧

Why did the chicken cross the road?
To avoid Colonel Sanders.

∧∧∧∧∧∧∧∧∧∧∧∧∧∧∧∧∧∧∧∧∧∧∧∧∧∧∧∧∧

Why did the chewing gum cross the road?
*It was stuck to the bottom of the chicken's
    shoe.*

∧∧∧∧∧∧∧∧∧∧∧∧∧∧∧∧∧∧∧∧∧∧∧∧∧∧∧∧∧

A chicken went to the doctor.
  "What's your problem?" the doctor
asked.
  "I have red, puffy spots all over my
skin."
  "Oh, no! You have the people pox!"

Why did the farmer cross the road?
To catch his chickens.

^^^^^^^^^^^^^^^^^^^^^^^^^^^^^^^^^^^^^

What's the best way to move a chicken?
Pullet.

^^^^^^^^^^^^^^^^^^^^^^^^^^^^^^^^^^^^^

Why did the brontosaurus
    cross the road?
*Chickens had not been
    invented.*

^^^^^^^^^^^^

"I don't like my job,"
grumbled the first rooster.
   "Why not?" asked the second rooster.
   "I'm working for chicken
feed."

Why do chickens have short legs?
So the eggs won't break as they're laid.

∧∧∧∧∧∧∧∧∧∧∧∧∧∧∧∧∧∧∧∧∧∧∧∧∧∧∧∧∧∧

Farmer: "Why aren't we having eggs for
breakfast this morning?"
Farmer's wife: "I think the chicken mislaid
them."

∧∧∧∧∧∧∧∧∧∧∧∧∧∧∧∧∧∧∧∧∧∧∧∧∧∧∧∧∧∧

What did the Navy get when it crossed a
chicken with a case of dynamite?
a mine layer.

∧∧∧∧∧∧∧∧∧∧∧∧∧∧∧∧∧∧∧∧∧∧∧∧∧∧∧∧∧∧

How do you catch a chicken?
*Hide in the yard and act like a corn
kernel.*

Who is the favorite actor of chickens?
Gregory Peck.

^^^^^^^^^^^^^^^^^^^^^^^^^^^^^^^

Why did the chicken go to New York City?
To visit the Henpire State Building.

^^^^^^^^^^^^^^^^^^^^^^^^^^^^^^^

What is the favorite musical of chickens?
*Fiddler on the
    Roost.*

^^^^^^^^^^^

How does a chicken
    farmer wake up
    in the morning?
*Probably with an alarm
    clock.*

Why did the rooster cluck at midnight?
His cluck was fast.

∧∧∧∧∧∧∧∧∧∧∧∧∧∧∧∧∧∧∧∧∧∧∧∧∧∧∧∧

Why did the rock band hire a chicken?
They needed the drumsticks.

∧∧∧∧∧∧∧∧∧∧∧∧∧∧∧∧∧∧∧∧∧∧∧∧∧∧∧∧

Why was the chicken sitting on the egg-
    plant?
She was nearsighted.

∧∧∧∧∧∧∧∧∧∧∧∧∧∧∧∧∧∧∧∧∧∧∧∧∧∧∧∧

How do chickens stay warm?
With their central bleating system.

CLOTHES

"Lane, look at you!" shrieked his mother. "You've ruined your brand new suit falling into the mud!"

"I'm sorry," Lane said. "I didn't have time to take it off before I hit the water."

^^^^^^^^^^^^^^^^^^^^^^^^^^^^^^^^^^^

Sherie: "Mommy, can I try on that dress in the window?"
Mother: "No, you'll have to go to the dressing room."

Why did Christy put on a wet dress?
Because the label said "Wash and Wear."

^^^^^^^^^^^^^^^^^^^^^^^^^^^^^^^^^^

Missy: "I just got a new pair of alligator
    shoes!"
Sissy: "I didn't know you had an alligator."

^^^^^^^^^^^^^^^^^^^^^^^^^^^^^^^^^^

Wren: "Don't you realize your umbrella has
    a hole in it?"
Adrienne: "Sure. It lets me check and see
    when the rain stops."

^^^^^^^^^^^^^^^^^^^^^^^^^^^^^^^^^^

Polly: "Why are you wearing all those
    clothes to go paint the fence?"
Agnes: "The can says you need two coats to
    do a good job."

CRAZY FOLKS

Why did the woman
remove her nose?
To see what made it run.

^^^^^^^^^^^^^^^^^^^^^^^^^^^^^^^^^^^^

Why did the carpenter put his finger over
the head of the nail he was hammering?
To muffle the noise.

Warren: "Lester sure has a weird sense of humor."

Katrina: "How so?"

Warren: "We went into an antique shop yesterday, and he asked the owner, 'What's new?' "

^^^^^^^^^^^^^^^^^^^^^^^^^^^^^^^^^^^

"Veronica has got to be the nicest person ever born," said Andrew.

"What makes you think so?" asked Arthur.

"She says 'thank you' to automatic sliding doors."

^^^^^^^^^^^^^^^^^^^^^^^^^^^^^^^^^^^

Dennis: "Steve's changed his mind again."

Suzanne: "Well, I hope this one's got more sense than the last one he had."

Susan: "We have a terrible problem. Our mother thinks she's a chicken."

Wanda: "Why don't you take her to a psychiatrist?"

Susan: "We need the eggs."

^^^^^^^^^^^^^^^^^^^^^^^^^^^^^^^^^^

Ray: "It's dark in here. Strike a match."

Roy: "I'm trying to, but this match won't light."

Ray: "Is it wet?"

Roy: "I don't think so. It worked a minute ago."

^^^^^^^^^^

Wilt: "You have a stately nose, sir."

Mort: "Why thank you. I picked it myself."

Michael: "Why are you making faces at my
    dog? That's silly."
Artie: "Well, he started it."

∧∧∧∧∧∧∧∧∧∧∧∧∧∧∧∧∧∧∧∧∧∧∧∧∧∧∧∧

Melissa: "I think Cathy's a little distracted.
    She sure is wasting a lot of money."
Sandi: "Oh? How?"
Melissa: "Well, for example, she's been
    going to a lot of drive-in movies lately."
Sandi: "That sounds pretty normal to me—
    and cheap."
Melissa: "But she takes a taxi."

∧∧∧∧∧∧∧∧∧∧∧∧∧∧∧∧∧∧∧∧∧∧∧∧∧∧∧∧

"My son thinks he's a dog. He barks at peo-
ple and chases cars and cats."
  "How long has he behaved this way?"
  "Basically, since he was a puppy."

DEFINITIONS

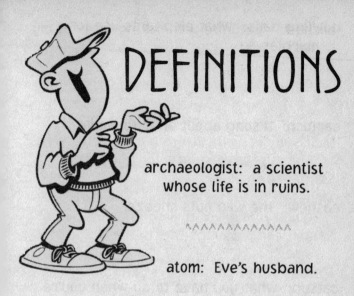

archaeologist: a scientist whose life is in ruins.

^^^^^^^^^^^^^

atom: Eve's husband.

^^^^^^^^^^^^^^^^^^^^^^^^^^^^^

autobiography: a book about a car.

^^^^^^^^^^^^^^^^^^^^^^^^^^^^

bookkeeper: a person who doesn't return library books on time.

bowling balls: what elephants use for
marbles.

∧∧∧∧∧∧∧∧∧∧∧∧∧∧∧∧∧∧∧∧∧∧∧∧∧∧∧∧∧

cartoon: a song about an automobile.

∧∧∧∧∧∧∧∧∧∧∧∧∧∧∧∧∧∧∧∧∧∧∧∧∧∧∧∧∧

cashew: the way nuts sneeze.

∧∧∧∧∧∧∧∧∧∧∧∧∧∧∧∧∧∧∧∧∧∧∧∧∧∧∧∧∧

catsup: what you have to do when you're
behind.

∧∧∧∧∧∧∧∧∧∧∧∧∧∧∧∧∧∧∧∧∧∧∧∧∧∧∧∧∧

Cheerios: what tiny people use for life
preservers.

Cheerios: donut seeds.

∧∧∧∧∧∧∧∧∧∧∧∧∧∧∧∧∧∧∧∧∧∧∧∧∧∧∧∧∧∧

chipmonk: a monkey eating potato
    chips.

∧∧∧∧∧∧∧∧∧∧∧∧∧∧∧∧∧∧∧∧∧∧∧∧∧∧∧∧

circle: a line that meets its other end in
    secret.

∧∧∧∧∧∧∧∧∧∧∧∧∧∧∧∧∧∧∧∧∧∧∧∧∧∧∧∧∧

commentator: an everyday potato.

∧∧∧∧∧

coquette: a
    small cola.

dentist's office: a filling station.

^^^^^^^^^^^^^^^^^^^^^^^^^^^^^^^^

disease: de seven big bodies of water
   where de ships sail.

^^^^^^^^^^^^^^^^^^^^^^^^^^^^^^^^

dogwood: the tree with the loudest bark.

^^^^^^^^^^^^^^^^^^^^^^^^^^^^^^^^

don't: short for "doughnut."

^^^^^^^^^^^^^^^^^^^^^^^^^^^^^^^^

drydock: a thirsty surgeon.

^^^^^^^^^^^^^^^^^^^^^^^^^^^^^^^^

enormous: a very large moose.

footnote: a sound you play with your feet.

^^^^^^^^^^^^^^^^^^^^^^^^^^^^^^^^^^^^

frozen police officers: copsicles.

^^^^^^^^^^^^^^^^^^^^^^^^^^^^^^^^^^^^

hippie: what holds up your leggie.

^^^^^^^^^^^^^^^^^^^^^^^^^^^^^^^^^^^^

horse doctor: a doctor with a sore throat.

^^^^^^^

humbug: a roach who loves music.

lambchops: the way sheep cut their fire-
wood.

∧∧∧∧∧∧∧∧∧∧∧∧∧∧∧∧∧∧∧∧∧∧∧∧∧∧∧∧

lemonade: helping a lemon cross the
street.

∧∧∧∧∧∧∧∧∧∧∧∧∧∧∧∧∧∧∧∧∧∧∧∧∧∧∧∧

mischief: the police chief's wife.

∧∧∧∧∧∧∧∧∧∧∧∧∧∧∧∧∧∧∧∧∧∧∧∧∧∧∧∧

mountain range: a cook stove inside a cabin
in the Rockies.

∧∧∧∧∧∧∧∧∧∧∧∧∧∧∧∧∧∧∧∧∧∧∧∧∧∧∧∧

mushroom: the room where Eskimos train
their sled dogs.

panther: a person who manufactures panths.

^^^^^^^^^^^^^^^^^^^^^^^^^^^^^^^^^

pineapple: the fruit of a pine tree.

^^^^^^^^^^^^^

pocket calculator: a device for counting pockets.

^^^^^^^^^^^^^^^^^^^

polygon: a deceased parrot.

^^^^^^^^^^^^^^^^^^

raisin: a worried grape.

short-order cook: a person who prepares
   food for children.

∧∧∧∧∧∧∧∧∧∧∧∧∧∧∧∧∧∧∧∧∧∧∧∧∧∧∧∧

stagecoach: a theatrical instructor.

∧∧∧∧∧∧∧∧∧∧∧∧∧∧∧∧∧∧∧∧∧∧∧∧∧∧∧∧

stucco: what happens when you step on a
   piece of used bubblegummo.

∧∧∧∧∧∧∧∧∧∧∧∧∧∧∧∧∧∧∧∧∧∧∧∧∧∧∧∧

Sugar Bowl: where flies play championship
   football.

∧∧∧∧∧∧∧∧∧∧∧∧∧∧∧∧∧∧∧∧∧∧∧∧∧∧∧∧

Super Bowl: swimming pool for Superman's
   goldfish.

teacher's pet: student of a teacher who can't afford a cat.

^^^^^^^^^^^^^^^^^^^^^^^^^^^^^^^^^^

thumb tacks: a tax on thumbs.

^^^^^^^^^^^^^^^^^^^^^^^^^^^^^^^^^^

toadstool: a place for a frog to sit down.

^^^^^^^^^^^^^^^^^^^^^^^^^^^^^^^^^^

unaware: what you put on first and take off last.

^^^^^^^^^^^

watershed: a haven for ships in the middle of the ocean.

venison: a type of meat that costs deerly.

^^^^^^^^^^^^^^^^^^^^^^^^^^^^^^^^^^^^^^^

vipers: the things that keep car vindows clear venever it rains.

^^^^^^^^^^^^^^^^^^^^^^^^^^^^^^^^^^^^^^^

waterbed: where fish sleep.

^^^^^^^^^^^^^^^^^^^^^^^^^^^^^^^^^^^^^^^

zebra: a horse in prison.

^^^^^^^^^^^^^^^^^^^^^^^^^^^^^^^^^^^^^^^

zinc: what happens to you in the water if you can't zwim.

DOCTORS

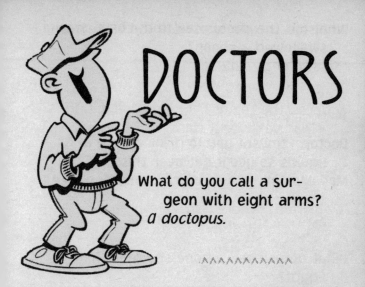

What do you call a surgeon with eight arms?
a doctopus.

ΛΛΛΛΛΛΛΛΛΛΛ

Patient: "Doc, can you make house calls?"
Doctor: "That depends. How sick is the house?"

ΛΛΛΛΛΛΛΛΛΛΛΛΛΛΛΛΛΛΛΛΛΛΛΛΛ

What kind of people enjoy bad health?
Doctors.

What did the doctor say to the woman who swallowed a spoon?
"Sit still and don't stir."

∧∧∧∧∧∧∧∧∧∧∧∧∧∧∧∧∧∧∧∧∧∧∧∧∧∧∧∧∧

Doctor: "I want you to drink plenty of liquids so you'll get over this cold."
Mrs. Martin: "I never drink anything else."

∧∧∧∧∧∧∧∧∧∧∧∧∧∧∧∧∧∧∧∧∧∧∧∧∧∧∧∧∧

What do you call a bone specialist from Egypt?
A Cairopractor.

∧∧∧∧∧∧∧∧∧∧∧∧∧∧∧∧∧∧∧∧∧∧∧∧∧∧∧∧∧

Eye Doctor: "You need a new pair of glasses."
Patient: "How do you know that? You haven't examined me yet."
Doctor: "Because you just came in through my office window."

How is a surgeon like a comedian?
They both keep you in stitches.

^^^^^^^^^^^^^^^^^^^^^^^^^^^^^^^^

A woman barged into a doctor's office and demanded attention.

"I dreamed I ate a giant marshmallow!" she screamed.

"Control yourself," said the receptionist. "It was only a dream."

"No dream! When I woke up, my pillow was missing!"

Woman: "My husband snores so loudly he keeps everybody in the house awake. What can we do?"

Doctor: "Try turning him on his side, massaging his shoulders and neck, and stuffing a washcloth into his mouth."

∧∧∧∧∧∧∧∧∧∧∧∧∧∧∧∧∧∧∧∧∧∧∧∧∧∧∧∧∧∧

What do you call foot X-rays?
Footographs.

ELEPHANTS

Why are elephants so
wrinkled?
*They stay in the bathtub
too long.*

∧∧∧∧∧∧∧∧∧∧

Why are elephants so wrinkled?
They're too difficult to iron.

∧∧∧∧∧∧∧∧∧∧∧∧∧∧∧∧∧∧∧∧∧∧∧∧∧

How do elephants communicate?
With elephones.

71

How do you make an elephant float?
Start with your favorite ice cream, pour cola over it and add elephant.

∧∧∧∧∧∧∧∧∧∧∧∧∧∧∧∧∧∧∧∧∧∧∧∧∧∧∧∧

Why is a snail small and smooth?
Because if it were huge and wrinkled, it would be an elephant.

∧∧∧∧∧∧∧∧∧∧∧∧∧∧∧∧∧∧∧∧∧∧∧∧∧∧∧∧

What's big and grey and has a trunk and goes 'zrrrrrrrrrrrr?'"
An outboard elephant.

∧∧∧∧∧∧∧∧∧∧∧∧∧∧∧∧∧∧∧∧∧∧∧∧∧∧∧∧

What's the difference between Superman and an elephant?
The elephant wears a big "E" on his chest.

Why was the elephant wearing a purple
    T-shirt?
His other shirts were all at the cleaners.

∧∧∧∧∧∧∧∧∧∧∧∧∧∧∧∧∧∧∧∧∧∧∧∧∧∧∧∧∧

How do you treat an elephant with sea-
    sickness?
Give it a lot of space.

∧∧∧∧∧∧∧∧∧∧∧∧∧∧∧∧∧∧∧∧∧∧∧∧∧∧∧∧∧

Why are
    elephants
    grey?
So you can tell them apart from bananas.

What's the best way to tell a kitten from an
  elephant?
*Try picking it up. If it's too heavy, it's surely
  an elephant.*

∧∧∧∧∧∧∧∧∧∧∧∧∧∧∧∧∧∧∧∧∧∧∧∧∧∧∧∧∧

What's the difference between an elephant
  in Africa and an elephant in India?
Several thousand miles.

FARM JOKES

One rooster said to another, "You don't want to mess with the new rooster in the yard. He's mean."

"How do you know?" asked the second rooster.

"He came from a hard-boiled egg."

^^^^^^^^^^^^^^^^^^^^^^^^^^^^^^^^^

What did the farmer say to the sheep?
"Hey, ewe!"

Mary was visiting her grandparents on the farm. "That little pig sure eats a lot of corn," she said.

"He has to make a hog of himself," said Grandmother, "or he'll never be full-grown."

∧∧∧∧∧∧∧∧∧∧∧∧∧∧∧∧∧∧∧∧∧∧∧∧∧∧∧∧∧

Why did the farmer put razor blades in the potato patch?
He wanted to grow potato chips.

∧∧∧∧∧∧∧∧∧∧∧∧∧∧∧∧∧∧∧∧∧∧∧∧∧∧

Farmer: "You know, the people in my little town are smarter than the people in your big city."
City Feller: "How do you get that?"
Farmer: "We know where LA is, but you don't know where Podunk is."

Why did the farmer spend the day stomping his field?
He wanted mashed potatoes.

^^^^^^^^^^^^^^^^^^^^^^^^^^^^^^^^^^^^

What did the farmer say to the hayfield?
"I'm very sorry, but I have to mow now."

^^^^^^^^^^^^^

What did the farmer do at the chocolate factory?
Milk chocolates.

^^^^^^^^^^^

What did the pea patch say to the corn patch?
Stop stalking me.

First farmer: "Did the tornado damage your barn last night?"

Second farmer: "I don't know. Haven't found it yet."

∧∧∧∧∧∧∧∧∧∧∧∧∧∧∧∧∧∧∧∧∧∧∧∧∧∧∧∧

Elaine: "My uncle just bought a farm that's a mile long and an inch wide.

Penny: "What does he think he can grow on land like that?"

Elaine: "Spaghetti, I guess."

∧∧∧∧∧∧∧∧∧∧∧∧∧∧∧∧∧∧∧∧∧∧∧∧∧∧∧∧

Betsy and Pat were roaming the meadows of their grandparents' farm when they encountered a dangerous-looking bull.

"Are you afraid?" asked Pat.

"Not me," said Betsy. "I'm a vegetarian."

Why did the farmer raise his children in a barn?
He wanted them to grow up in a stable environment.

^^^^^^^^^^^^^^^^^^^^^^^^^^^^^^^^^^^^^^

When do you hear the shout, "Ready. . . . Set. . . .Hoe?"
At the beginning of a race between two farmers.

^^^^^^

Robby: "What would you do if a bull charged?"
Toby: "I'd give him all the time he wanted to pay off the bill."

FOOD

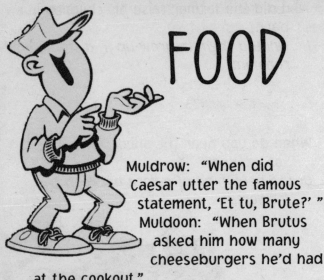

Muldrow: "When did Caesar utter the famous statement, 'Et tu, Brute?' "
Muldoon: "When Brutus asked him how many cheeseburgers he'd had at the cookout."

^^^^^^^^^^^^^^^^^^^^^^^^^^^^^^

Coreen: "I ate a yo-yo lunch."
Sonny: "What's a yo-yo lunch?"
Coreen: "Soon after you get it down, it comes up again."

What did one hot dog say to the other?
"Frankly, I prefer cheeseburgers."

∧∧∧∧∧∧∧∧∧∧∧∧∧∧∧∧∧∧∧∧∧∧∧∧∧∧∧∧

What's the difference between a jar of
    peanut butter and a freight
    train?
*a freight train doesn't stick to
    the roof of your mouth.*

∧∧∧∧∧∧∧∧∧∧∧∧∧∧∧∧∧

How do you deliver fried
    pies to customers?
On piecycles.

∧∧∧∧∧∧∧∧∧∧∧

Why was Miss Muffet
    reading a map?
*Because she'd lost her
    whey.*

What's the favorite food of Martians?
Martianmallows.

∧∧∧∧∧∧∧∧∧∧∧∧∧∧∧∧∧∧∧∧∧∧∧∧∧∧∧∧∧∧∧

What's the difference between an Oreo
cookie and a cheeseburger?
Oreos taste much better dunked in milk.

∧∧∧∧∧∧∧∧∧∧∧∧∧∧∧∧∧∧∧∧∧∧∧∧∧∧∧∧∧∧∧

One Irish potato said to the other Irish
potato, "I'm about to change my
nationality."
  "How are you going to do that?"
  "By becoming French fries."

∧∧∧∧∧∧∧∧∧∧∧∧∧∧∧∧∧∧∧∧∧∧∧∧∧∧∧∧∧∧∧

Ingrid: "Do you know what makes the Tower
of Pisa lean?"
Peter: "It's malnourished, I guess."

How do you tell a chili pepper from a bell pepper?
The chili pepper always wears a jacket.

^^^^^^^^^^^^^^^^^^^^^^^^^^^^^^^^^

What did one cannibal say to the other as they gobbled up a clown?
"This food tastes funny."

^^^^^^^^^^^

What's the favorite lunch item in Iceland?
Chili dogs.

^^^^^^^^^

What happened when Grandma served ostrich instead of turkey for Thanksgiving dinner?
It buried its head in the pumpkin pie.

Father: "It's proper manners to eat your
food with your fork, not your spoon."
Marvin: "But my fork leaks."

∧∧∧∧∧∧∧∧∧∧∧∧∧∧∧∧∧∧∧∧∧∧∧∧∧∧∧∧

A prospector straggled into town, went
into the little cafe and told the owner,
"Buddy, I'm starved almost to death.
It's been two weeks since I've tasted food."
  The bartender responded, "Well, it all
tastes about the same as it did back
then."

∧∧∧∧∧∧∧∧∧∧∧∧∧∧∧∧∧∧∧∧∧∧∧∧∧∧∧∧

Chris: "I have to eat very balanced
meals."
Burt: "I didn't know you were so health-
conscious."
Chris: "I'm not, really. I'm training to be a
tightrope walker."

Thomas: "Gerald sure does love Chinese food."

Veronica: "Yeah, I think he's a chow meiniac."

^^^^^^^^^^^^^^^^^^^^^^^^^^^^^^^^

Rene: "How do you like those crab-apples?"

Richard: "They taste rather salty, for apples."

^^^^^^^^^^^

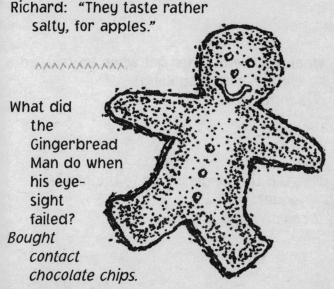

What did the Gingerbread Man do when his eye-sight failed?

Bought contact chocolate chips.

Teacher: "Marvin, you haven't washed. I can see food on your face."

Marvin: "What food?"

Teacher: "The eggs you had for breakfast this morning."

Marvin: "Eggs? I had cereal for breakfast this morning. The eggs must be from yesterday morning."

∧∧∧∧∧∧∧∧∧∧∧∧∧∧∧∧∧∧∧∧∧∧∧∧∧∧∧∧∧

What did the butcher get when he crossed a chicken with King Kong?

a giant drumstick.

∧∧∧∧∧∧∧∧∧∧∧∧∧∧∧∧∧∧∧∧∧∧∧∧∧∧∧∧∧

Why did the tangerine go to the movies alone?

It couldn't find a date.

Maria: "You can have my M&Ms."
Alex: "You don't like candy?"
Maria: "Not this kind. Too hard to peel."

^^^^^^^^^^^^^^^^^^^^^^^^^^^^^^^^^^^

How can you tell if a rattle-
   snake has been
   drinking your
   milk?
*By the two fang
marks in the
carton.*

^^^^^^^^

What do you get if you
   cross a bulldog with
   a bull?
*A burger that can bite
back.*

FROGS

What goes "CROAK!
CROAK!" on foggy nights?
a froghorn.

∧∧∧∧∧∧∧∧∧∧∧

What's green and stands in a
corner?
a frog that got caught talking in class.

∧∧∧∧∧∧∧∧∧∧∧∧∧∧∧∧∧∧∧∧∧∧∧∧∧∧∧

What's white on the outside, green on the
inside and makes croaking sounds?
a frog sandwich.

GROWN-UPS

"I think my father's getting old," Keri lamented.

"What makes you think so?" asked Janelle.

"It takes him more time to rest up than it does to get tired."

^^^^^^^^^^^^^^^^^^^^^^^^^^^^^^^^^

Sally: "My mother has trained herself to walk in her sleep every night."

Cal: "Why would she want to do that?"

Sally: "To save time. This way she can get her exercise and her rest all at once."

"Grandpa, why don't you ever read the newspaper?"

"I don't want to put any needless wear on my spectacles."

∧∧∧∧∧∧∧∧∧∧∧∧∧∧∧∧∧∧∧∧∧∧∧∧∧∧∧∧∧

Grandma was giving Sarah some wise advice: "Never put off until tomorrow what you can do today. Do you understand what I mean?"

"Yes, Grandma. It means we should finish this apple pie right now."

∧∧∧∧∧∧∧∧∧∧∧∧∧∧∧∧∧∧∧∧∧∧∧∧∧∧∧∧∧

"I don't think my mom is a very smart parent," Jill said.

"Why not?" asked Grace Ann.

"She's always sending me to bed when I'm not sleepy and making me get up when I'm still tired."

Patti: "How do you do today?"
Grumpy Grandpa: "How do I do what?"

∧∧∧∧∧∧∧∧∧∧∧∧∧∧∧∧∧∧∧∧∧∧∧∧∧∧∧∧∧

Kendra: "Martin, what will you do when you
grow up to be as big as your daddy?"
Martin: "Go on a diet, first of all."

∧∧∧∧∧∧∧∧∧∧∧

Don: "My parents
once crossed
the Atlantic
with Elizabeth
on the Queen
Elizabeth II."
Dean: "You mean
they got to
know the
queen?"
Don: "No, they
were with my Grandmother Elizabeth."

91

Some grown-ups are as hard to wake up as
sleeping bags.

∧∧∧∧∧∧∧∧∧∧∧∧∧∧∧∧∧∧∧∧∧∧∧∧∧∧∧∧

Bailey: "Why does your dad wrap news-
papers all over himself?"
Barry: "He likes to dress with *The Times*."

∧∧∧∧∧∧∧∧∧∧∧∧∧∧∧∧∧∧∧∧∧∧∧∧∧∧∧

Why did Mommy tip-toe past the medicine
cabinet?
*She didn't want to wake up the sleeping
pills.*

∧∧∧∧∧∧∧∧∧∧∧∧∧∧∧∧∧∧∧∧∧∧∧∧∧∧∧∧

Mother: "Stan, wash your face."
Stan: "It's not fair."
Mother: "What do you mean?"
Stan: "Dad has less to wash because of his
beard."

"I figured out how to make my dad laugh on Sunday."

"Really? How?"

"I told him a joke Friday."

∧∧∧∧∧∧∧∧∧∧∧∧∧∧∧∧∧∧∧∧∧∧∧∧∧∧

Mother: "Troy, I've been calling you for the last five minutes! Didn't you hear me?"

Troy: "No, I didn't hear you until the fourth time you called."

∧∧∧∧∧∧∧∧∧∧∧∧∧

David: "My dad never gets his hair wet when he showers."

Nan: "Does he wear a shower cap?"

David: "Nope. He's bald."

93

"Mom, may I go upstairs and play with the guinea pig?" Daniel asked.

"Why son, why would you want to see a guinea pig when Grandmom is here visiting?"

ΛΛΛΛΛΛΛΛΛΛΛΛΛΛΛΛΛΛΛΛΛΛΛΛΛΛΛΛΛΛ

"My grandmother is always complaining about how awful it feels to be old," Carmen said.

"Mine, too," said Dixie. "I guess those wrinkles hurt a lot."

ΛΛΛΛΛΛΛΛΛΛΛΛΛΛΛΛΛΛΛΛΛΛΛΛΛΛΛΛΛΛ

Sal: "I can't think of a good present for Mom on Mother's Day."

Val: "Why not lipstick?"

Sal: "Nah. . . .I'm not sure what size her mouth is."

"Do you get spanked much?" a child asked his friend.

"Yes. I think I'm the kind of boy my parents don't want me to play with."

∧∧∧∧∧∧∧∧∧∧∧∧∧∧∧∧∧∧∧∧∧∧∧∧∧∧∧∧∧

Rachel: "Do you know the difference between Daddy's toys and our brother's toys?"
Fran: "Yeah, Daddy's cost a lot more money."

∧∧∧∧∧∧∧∧∧∧∧∧

Earl: "Wanna know a funny coincidence about my parents?"
Virl: "Sure. What?"
Earl: "They were both married at the same time, same day, same year—and same place!"

HISTORY

Why did Columbus sail to America?
   It was faster than swimming.

vΛΛΛΛΛΛΛΛΛΛ

Why did cave men live in caves?
They couldn't afford condominiums.

ΛΛΛΛΛΛΛΛΛΛΛΛΛΛΛΛΛΛΛΛΛΛΛΛΛΛΛΛΛ

Why did the Romans build straight roads?
*So their enemies couldn't hide around the
   curves.*

Teacher: "How long did the Hundred Years' War last?"

Student: "I don't know. Ten years?"

Teacher: "No! Think carefully. How old is a 5-year-old horse?"

Student, thoughtfully: "Oh, 5 years old!"

Teacher: "That's right. So how long did the Hundred Years' War last?"

Student: "Now I get it—5 years!"

∧∧∧∧∧∧∧∧∧∧∧∧

The teacher held up a picture of Abraham Lincoln and asked the class, "Can anyone tell me who this is?"

"I know!" shouted Mindy. "He's the man who owns all the pennies."

History Teacher: "What English monarch was also an amateur doctor?"

Jamie: "William the Corn Curer?"

∧∧∧∧∧∧∧∧∧∧∧∧∧∧∧∧∧∧∧∧∧∧∧∧∧∧∧∧∧∧

Teacher: "What was the Romans' most famous achievement?"

Pupil: "They could read Latin."

∧∧∧∧∧∧∧∧∧∧∧∧∧∧∧∧∧∧∧∧∧∧∧∧∧∧∧∧∧∧

History Teacher: "Now Wally, what can you tell us about President Millard Fillmore?"

Wally: "He's dead."

∧∧∧∧∧∧∧∧∧∧∧∧∧∧∧∧∧∧∧∧∧∧∧∧∧∧∧∧∧∧

Baker: "I wish I'd been born about 4,000 years ago."

Brewster: "Why?"

Baker: "So I wouldn't have to learn so much history."

How did the ancient Vikings communicate?
Norse Code.

∧∧∧∧∧∧∧∧∧∧∧∧∧∧∧∧∧∧∧∧∧∧∧∧∧∧∧∧

A history teacher was discussing the early American explorers. "Merrivale the Monk spent years living with the native Americans, learning their songs," she said. "The Indians gave him a special name. Do you know what it was, Jack?"

"Tone-Deaf," guessed Jack.

∧∧∧∧∧∧∧∧∧∧∧∧∧

Where did Lincoln sign the Emancipation Proclamation?
At the bottom of the last page.

Teacher: "Who won at Bull Run?"
Student: "Was that a tennis match or a
   horse race?"

^^^^^^^^^^^^^^^^^^^^^^^^^^^^^^^^^^^

Lana: "My great-great-great-grandparents
   were the first citizens of this town."
Kurt: "That's nothing. My ancestors fought
   in the Revolutionary War."
Lana: "My ancestors fought in ancient
   Rome."
Kurt: "My ancestors fought for Alexander
   the Great before that."
Lana: "My ancestors were on the ark with
   Noah."
Kurt: "My ancestors had their own ship."

^^^^^^^^^^^^^^^^^^^^^^^^^^^^^^^^^^^

What do history teachers talk about when
   they get together?
The old days.

William: "Did you hear the North and South are going to refight the Battle of Kennesaw Mountain?"

Wade: "What for?"

William: "Because it wasn't fought on the level the first time."

^^^^^^^^^^^^^^^^^^^^^^^^^^^^^^^^

Teacher: "What do you think George Washington would say about America if he were alive today?"

Student: "Doesn't matter. He would be so old, his ideas would be completely useless."

HOUSES

Two carpenters were building a house. One examined every nail before using it and ended up throwing half of them away.

"Why are you wasting those nails?" his partner asked.

"They're no good. The sharp points are on the wrong end."

"Yeah, but you could use those for the other side of the house.

Marcia: "How do you like your new house?"

Kyle: "It's okay, but kinda small. We had to remove the paint from the walls in order to make all our furniture fit."

∧∧∧∧∧∧∧∧∧∧∧∧∧∧∧∧∧∧∧∧∧∧∧∧∧∧∧∧∧∧∧∧∧

Dee Dee: "Did you know Santa Claus has a secret fear of crawling down chim- neys?"

Pee Wee: "No! Is he afraid of closed-in places?"

Dee Dee: "Yes. It's called Claustrophobia."

KITCHEN JOKES

Ginger: "Mommy, I need another glass of milk."

Mommy: "You've had two already. Why are you so thirsty this morning?"

Ginger: "I'm not. I'm checking to see if my throat leaks."

^^^^^^^^^^^^^^^^^^^^^^^^^^^^^^^^^^^^^

How do goblins order their eggs?
Horrifried.

Mother: "Joy, haven't you finished making the Kool-Aid yet?"

Joy: "I'm having trouble getting the water into the envelope."

∧∧∧∧∧∧∧∧∧∧∧∧∧∧∧∧∧∧∧∧∧∧∧∧∧∧∧∧∧∧

Where do hot dogs dance?
At meatballs.

∧∧∧∧∧∧∧∧∧∧∧∧∧∧∧∧∧∧∧

What are the four seasons?
Salt, pepper, catsup, and mayonnaise.

∧∧∧∧∧∧∧∧∧∧∧∧∧∧∧∧

How can you tell if there's a horse in your refrigerator?
By the hoofprints in the butter.

Beth: "Would you like to join me in a cup of tea?"

Veronica: "I don't think we'd both fit."

∧∧∧∧∧∧∧∧∧∧∧∧∧∧∧∧∧∧∧∧∧∧∧∧∧∧∧∧∧

Liz: "My mom's not a very good cook."

Trish: "Does breakfast taste awful?"

Liz: "No, just weird. She can't even get a pop tart out of the toaster in one piece."

∧∧∧∧∧∧∧∧∧∧∧∧∧∧∧∧∧∧∧∧∧∧∧∧∧∧∧∧∧

How do you repair a broken casserole dish?
With tomato paste.

∧∧∧∧∧∧∧∧∧∧∧∧∧∧∧∧∧∧∧∧∧∧∧∧∧∧∧∧∧

What did Mary have for supper?
a little lamb.

Paul: "Why are you staring at that frozen orange juice can?"

Donna: "Can't you see? It says 'concentrate.'"

^^^^^^^^^^^^^^^^^^^^^^^^^^^^^^^

Mom, entering the kitchen: "I see you've been making chocolate chip cookies."

Marsha: "Can you smell them in the oven already?"

Mom: "No, but I notice M&M shells all over the floor."

^^^^^^^^^^^^^^^^^^^

What ice cream dessert is brown, white and red?
a chocolate sundae with catsup.

KNOCK-KNOCK JOKES

Knock-knock.
   Who's there?
Howie.
   Howie Who?
Howie gonna win the baseball game if you
   won't come out and play?

Knock-knock.
   Who's there?
Butcher.
   Butcher Who?
Butcher hands up! This is a robbery!

^^^^^^^^^^^^^^^^^^^^^^^^^^^^^

Knock-knock.
   Who's there?
Abbey.
   Abbey Who?
Abbey birthday to
   you. . . .

^^^^^^^^^

Knock-knock.
   Who's there?
Howard.
   Howard Who?
Howard is it to lift a
   piano?

Knock-knock.
  Who's there?
Dune.
  Dune Who?
Dune anything in particular this afternoon?

∧∧∧∧∧∧∧∧∧∧∧∧∧∧∧∧∧∧∧∧∧∧∧∧∧∧∧

Knock-knock.
  Who's there?
Pasta.
  Pasta Who?
Pasta gravy, please.

∧∧∧∧∧∧∧∧∧∧∧∧∧∧∧∧∧∧∧∧∧∧∧∧∧∧∧

Knock-knock.
  Who's there?
Luke.
  Luke Who?
Luke at me twirl my Hoola-Hoop!

Knock-knock.
  Who's there?
Irish.
  Irish Who?
Irish you would open the door.

^^^^^^^^^^^^^^^^^^^^^^^^^^^^^^^^^

Knock-knock.
  Who's there?
Peas.
  Peas Who?
Peas open the door and let
  me in.

^^^^^^^^^^^

Knock-knock.
  Who's there?
Snakeskin.
  Snakeskin Who?
Snakeskin hurtchew, if you ain't keerful.

Knock-knock.
   Who's there?
Fanny.
   Fanny Who?
Fannybody wants to come out and play, I'm
   waiting.

∧∧∧∧∧∧∧∧∧∧∧∧∧∧∧∧∧∧∧∧∧∧∧∧∧∧∧∧∧∧

Knock-knock.
   Who's there?
Tock.
   Tock Who?
Tock to me. I'm lonely.

∧∧∧∧∧∧∧∧∧∧∧∧∧∧∧∧∧∧∧∧∧∧∧∧∧∧∧∧∧∧

Knock-knock.
   Who's there?
Cinnamon.
   Cinnamon Who?
Cinnamon dressed in blue pass by here
   lately?

Knock-knock.
 Who's there?
Staten Island.
 Staten Island Who?
Staten Island I see out there in the water?

∧∧∧∧∧∧∧∧∧∧∧∧∧∧∧∧∧∧∧∧∧∧∧∧∧∧∧∧∧∧

Knock-knock.
 Who's there?
Midas.
 Midas Who?
Midas well let me in.
 I'm not going any-
 where.

∧∧∧∧∧∧∧∧∧∧

Knock-knock.
 Who's there?
Arthur.
 Arthur Who?
Arthur any mean dogs around here?

Knock-knock.
    Who's there?
Phillip.
    Phillip Who?
Phillip the dog's water bowl, please. He's
    very thirsty.

∧∧∧∧∧∧∧∧∧∧∧∧∧∧∧∧∧∧∧∧∧∧∧∧∧∧∧∧∧∧∧

Knock-knock.
    Who's there?
Matthews.
    Matthews Who?
Matthews are wet. Can I come in and dwy
    my thocks?

∧∧∧∧∧∧∧∧∧∧∧∧∧∧∧∧∧∧∧∧∧∧∧∧∧∧∧∧∧∧∧

Knock-knock.
    Who's there?
Rhoda.
    Rhoda Who?
Rhoda letter to my mama today.

Knock-knock.
  Who's there?
Owl.
  Owl Who?
Owl tell you if promise not to reveal my
  owdentity.

∧∧∧∧∧∧∧∧∧∧∧∧∧∧∧∧∧∧∧∧∧∧∧∧∧∧∧∧∧

Knock-knock.
  Who's there?
Lena.
  Lena Who?
Lena little closer. I
  don't hear too good.

∧∧∧∧∧∧∧∧∧∧∧∧∧

Knock-knock.
  Who's there?
Watson.
  Watson Who?
Watson the grill? I'm hungry.

Knock-knock.
    Who's there?
Fido.
    Fido Who?
Fido known you lived here, I'do come to visit
    sooner.

∧∧∧∧∧∧∧∧∧∧∧∧∧∧∧∧∧∧∧∧∧∧∧∧∧∧∧∧

Knock-knock.
    Who's there?
Dishes.
    Dishes Who?
Dishes Tommy, your besht friend. Don't you
    recognishe me?

∧∧∧∧∧∧∧∧∧∧∧∧∧∧∧∧∧∧∧∧∧∧∧∧∧∧∧∧

Knock-knock.
    Who's there?
Samoa.
    Samoa Who?
Samoa ice kweam, pwease.

Knock-knock.
  Who's there?
Sarah.
  Sarah Who?
Sarah good way for me to untie this knot?

^^^^^^^^^^^^^^^^^^^^^^^^^^^^^^^^

Knock-knock.
  Who's there?
Juneau.
  Juneau Who?
Juneau I was your next-
  door neighbor?

^^^^^^^

Knock-knock.
  Who's
  there?
Jamaica.
  Jamaica Who?
Jamaica hotdog for me if I asked you to?

Knock-knock.
　　Who's there?
Wendy.
　　Wendy Who?
Wendy come looking for me, tell them I'm not
　　here.

^^^^^^^^^^^^^^^^^^^^^^^^^^^^^^^^^^

Knock-knock.
　　Who's there?
Celeste.
　　Celeste Who?
Celeste time I'll ever ask you to come out
　　and play.

^^^^^^^^^^^^^^^^^^^^^^^^^^^^^^^^^^

Knock-knock.
　　Who's there?
Lettuce.
　　Lettuce Who?
Lettuce in! It's raining out here!

Knock-knock.
  Who's there?
Ken.
  Ken Who?
Ken you come out and play this afternoon?

^^^^^^^^^^^^^^^^^^^^^^^^^^^^^^^^

Knock-knock.
  Who's there?
Bewitches.
  Bewitches Who?
Bewitches in just a moment.

^^^^^^^^^

Knock-knock.
  Who's there?
Turnip.
  Turnip Who?
Turnip the
  stereo,
  please.

Knock-knock.
　　Who's there?
Sherwood.
　　Sherwood Who?
Sherwood like to play with y'all this after-
　　noon.

∧∧∧∧∧∧∧∧∧∧∧∧∧∧∧∧∧∧∧∧∧∧∧∧∧∧∧∧

Knock-knock.
　　Who's there?
Sam.
　　Sam Who?
Sam times I think you don't love me lak I
　　love you.

∧∧∧∧∧∧∧∧∧∧∧∧∧∧∧∧∧∧∧∧∧∧∧∧∧∧∧∧

Knock-knock.
　　Who's there?
Police.
　　Police Who?
Police open the door.

Knock-knock.
   Who's there?
Kenya.
   Kenya Who?
Kenya gimme a dollar to buy an ice cream
   cone?

∧∧∧∧∧∧∧∧∧∧∧∧∧∧∧∧∧∧∧∧∧∧∧∧∧∧∧∧∧∧∧

Knock-knock.
   Who's there?
Jess.
   Jess Who?
Jess open the door and don't ask questions.

∧∧∧∧∧∧∧∧∧∧∧∧

Knock-knock.
   Who's there?
Annette.
   Annette Who?
Annette catches
   more fish than a hook.

Knock-knock.
   Who's there?
Anita.
   Anita Who?
Anita flashlight so I can see in the dark.

∧∧∧∧∧∧∧∧∧∧∧∧∧∧∧∧∧∧∧∧∧∧∧∧∧∧∧∧

Knock, Knock.
   Who's there?
Thumping.
   Thumping who?
Thumping fuzzy and gross is crawling down
   your back.

∧∧∧∧∧∧∧∧∧∧∧∧∧∧∧∧∧∧∧∧∧∧∧∧∧∧∧∧

Knock-knock.
   Who's there?
Noise.
   Noise Who?
Noise day, isn't it?

Knock-knock.
   Who's there?
Alaska.
   Alaska Who?
Alaska my dad if I can come outta play.

^^^^^^^^^^

Knock-knock.
   Who's there?
Stan.
   Stan Who?
Stan back. I'm
   coming in.

^^^^^^^^^^

Knock-knock.
   Who's there?
Max.
   Max Who?
Max me hungry just
   smellin' those hamburgers on the grill.

Knock-knock.
   Who's there?
Telephone.
   Telephone Who?
Telephone company they've made a mistake
   on our long-distance bill.

∧∧∧∧∧∧∧∧∧∧∧∧∧∧∧∧∧∧∧∧∧∧∧∧∧∧

Knock-knock.
   Who's there?
Dishwashing.
   Dishwashing Who?
Dishwashing the way I ushed to shpeak
   before I losht my two front teeth.

∧∧∧∧∧∧∧∧∧∧∧∧∧∧∧∧∧∧∧∧∧∧∧∧∧∧

Knock-knock.
   Who's there?
Abyssinia.
   Abyssinia Who?
Abyssinia in church Sunday.

124

Knock-knock.
   Who's there?
Theresa.
   Theresa Who?
Theresa thunderstorm coming up; close the
   windows.

∧∧∧∧∧∧∧∧∧∧∧∧∧∧∧∧∧∧∧∧∧∧∧∧∧∧∧

Knock-knock.
   Who's there?
Moscow.
   Moscow Who?
Moscow is brown and
   pa's cow is
   black with
   horns.

∧∧∧∧∧∧∧∧

Knock-knock.
   Who's there?
Sam the drummer.
   Beat it.

Knock-knock.
　Who's there?
Adolph.
　Adolph Who?
Adolph ball just came in the window.

∧∧∧∧∧∧∧∧∧∧∧∧∧∧∧∧∧∧∧∧∧∧∧∧∧∧

Knock-knock.
　Who's there?
Pudding.
　Pudding Who?
Just pudding the final touches on painting
　your door.

∧∧∧∧∧∧∧∧∧∧∧∧∧∧∧∧∧∧∧∧∧∧∧∧∧∧

Knock-knock.
　Who's there?
Warts.
　Warts Who?
Warts the difference between frogs and
　toads?

MUSIC

Adam: "I crossed a dog with a piano student."

Vera: "What did you get?"

Adam: "A dog whose bark was worse than her bite."

^^^

Claire: "Those are cute bongos you have for earrings. They're so tiny! Can you really play them?"

Brittany: "Yes. Those are my ear drums."

Who was the spiciest rock 'n' roll singer of
    all time?
Elvis Parsley.

∧∧∧∧∧∧∧∧∧∧∧∧∧∧∧∧∧∧∧∧∧∧∧∧∧∧∧∧∧

Patrice: "What's a hobo?"
Nicole: "I think it's a wind instrument."

∧∧∧∧∧∧∧∧∧∧∧∧∧∧∧∧∧∧∧∧∧∧∧∧∧∧∧∧∧

Meredith: "I've been playing the piano for
    five years now."
Ethan: "Do you ever stop to go to the bath-
    room?"

∧∧∧∧∧∧∧∧∧∧∧∧∧∧∧∧∧∧∧∧∧∧∧∧∧∧∧∧∧

Sheila: "Why does Francis Scott Key get
    credit for 'The Star-Spangled Banner?' "
Richie: "I guess because he learned all the
    words before anyone else."

Why was the lemon banned from the orchestra?
It hit too many sour notes.

∧∧∧∧∧∧∧∧∧∧∧∧∧∧∧∧∧∧∧∧∧∧∧∧∧

What did the pianist do after his wrists developed Carpal Tunnel Syndrome?
Played by ear.

∧∧∧∧∧∧∧∧∧∧∧∧

What brass instrument is twice as large as a tuba?
A fourba.

∧∧∧∧∧∧∧∧∧∧∧

Erskine: "I think I need to clean my tuba."
Band Director: "Try this tuba toothpaste."

How do you keep your arm from going to
   sleep?
Wear a singing wristwatch.

ΛΛΛΛΛΛΛΛΛΛΛΛΛΛΛΛΛΛΛΛΛΛΛΛΛΛΛ

Patient: "I've swallowed my harmonica."
Doctor: "Good thing you don't play the
   guitar."

ΛΛΛΛΛΛΛΛΛΛΛΛΛΛΛΛΛΛΛΛΛΛΛΛΛΛΛ

"I know a woman who can sing alto and
soprano at the same time."
   "How does she do that?"
   "She has two heads."

ΛΛΛΛΛΛΛΛΛΛΛΛΛΛΛΛΛΛΛΛΛΛΛΛΛΛΛ

What's a geologist's favorite kind of music?
Rock.

Clive: "It sure was an interesting symphony
concert last night. The tuba player's wig
slid off into the bell of his horn!"

Harry: "Oh, no! Did they stop the concert?"

Clive: "No. He just blew his top and went
right on playing."

^^^^^^^^^^^^^^^

Steven: "I wish you
sang only
Christmas
carols."

Mickey: "Why?"

Steven: "Then
I'd have to
listen to you only
one month out of
the year."

OCCUPATIONS

Reporter: "Do you like your job, sir?"
Astronomer: "Yes. It's heavenly."

^^^^^^^^^^^^^^^

How do preachers communicate with each other?
Parson to parson.

^^^^^^^^^^^^^^^^^^^^^^^^^^^

Where do FBI agents go on vacation?
Club Fed.

OCEANS & RIVERS

Albert: "Do you know what happens when you throw a grey rock into the Red Sea?"

Lon: "It changes color?"

Albert: "No, it gets wet."

^^^^^^^^^^^^^^^^^^^^^^^^^^^^^^^^^^

What was Moby Dick's favorite dinner?
Fish and ships.

133

The Cantrell family were vacationing aboard a Mississippi River steamboat.

"Is it true," little brother asked the steamboat captain, "that you know every stump and snag on the whole Mississippi River?"

"I sure do," the captain boasted.

Just then the boat ran up on a snag and stopped abruptly.

"There's one," the captain said.

PLAYING

Jacqui strolled into the kitchen with a brand new baseball.

"Where did you get that?" her mother asked.

"Outside. It was lost."

"Now Jacqui, are you sure it was lost?"

"Yeah, I saw the boy down the street looking for it."

^^^^^^^^^^^^^^^^^^^^^^^^^^^^^^^

Mother: "Charlie, why aren't you playing ball with your friends?"

Charlie: "Every time it's my turn, they change the rules."

135

Bart: "Your nose is red. You must've been in the sun too long at the beach yesterday."

Shane: "No I wasn't. I was bobbing for French fries."

^^^^^^^^^^^^^^^^^^^^^^^^^^^^^^^^^

Swimmer: "Are there any sharks in this bay?"

Lifeguard: "Not anymore. The crocodiles got 'em."

^^^^^^^^^^^^^^^^^^^^^^^^^^^^^^^^^

A mother came home to find the living room window broken. "Joel," she called to her son, "do you know anything about this window?"

"Well," Joel said, "I was cleaning my slingshot, and it went off accidentally."

RESTAURANTS

Marsha: "Did you hear about the new café in Paris that sells bag lunches?"

Amy: "No. What's it called?"

Marsha: "The Lunch Bag of Notre Dame."

^^^^^^^^^^^^^^^^^^^^^^^^^^^^^^^^^^^^^

Walker: "This is not a very good restaurant. I just found a bone."

Suzette: "In your soup?"

Walker: "No, in my lasagna."

What's the best way for a guy to propose to a gal at a fast-food restaurant?
With an onion ring.

∧∧∧∧∧∧∧∧∧∧∧∧∧∧∧∧∧∧∧∧∧∧∧∧∧∧∧∧

Waitress: "Would you like for me to cut your pizza into four pieces or eight?"
Dawn: "Four. We'd never finish eight."

∧∧∧∧∧∧∧∧∧∧∧∧∧∧∧∧∧∧∧∧∧∧∧∧∧∧∧∧

Waiter: "Did you enjoy your bison steaks?"
Dining family, in unison: "Yes, we enjoyed them very much!"
Waiter: "Good. Here's your buffalo bill."

∧∧∧∧∧∧∧∧∧∧∧∧∧∧∧∧∧∧∧∧∧∧∧∧∧∧∧∧

Amy: "Did you know NASA has opened a café on the surface of the moon?"
Marsha: "Yeah. I heard it has no atmosphere to speak of."

Rich Diner: "What's the most expensive soup you have on the menu?"

Waitress: "The one with six carrots in it."

∧∧∧∧∧∧∧∧∧∧∧∧∧∧∧∧∧∧∧∧∧∧∧∧∧∧∧∧

A dog walked into a restaurant, sat down at a table and ordered a cup of coffee.

"That'll be a dollar," the waitress said when she brought the coffee. She added, "You're the first dog I've ever served coffee."

"And at a dollar a cup," said the dog, "I'm sure I'll be the last."

∧∧∧∧∧∧∧∧∧∧

Who was the restaurant's star waiter?
Souperman.

139

It was almost closing time, and the ice cream parlor was running very low on supplies when a crowd of teenagers came in after a soccer game.

"What flavors do you have?" asked one.

"Chocolate, vanilla, strawberry, peach and cherry," said the clerk. "And you can have any one you want, as long as it's vanilla."

∧∧∧∧∧∧∧∧∧∧∧∧∧∧∧∧∧∧∧∧∧∧∧∧∧∧∧∧

Two girls went into a fast-food restaurant late one night.

"Have you got anymore cheeseburgers?" asked one.

"Sure," said the clerk.

"Then why did you make so many?"

RIDDLES

What's the most successful thing government has ever invented? *The postage stamp, because it always sticks to its task until completion.*

∧∧∧∧∧∧∧∧∧∧∧∧∧∧∧∧∧∧∧∧∧∧∧∧∧∧∧∧

Teacher: "If four people are standing beneath one umbrella, how many do you think will get wet?"
Student: *"Depends on whether it's raining."*

What are ten things in life you can always count on?
Your fingers.

∧∧∧∧∧∧∧∧∧∧∧∧∧∧∧∧∧∧∧∧∧∧∧∧∧∧∧∧

What kind of ears do you find on a train engine?
Engineers.

∧∧∧∧∧∧∧∧∧∧∧∧∧∧∧∧∧∧∧∧∧∧∧∧∧∧∧∧

What can you break just by calling its name?
Silence.

∧∧∧∧∧∧∧∧∧∧∧∧∧∧∧∧∧∧∧∧∧∧∧∧∧∧∧∧

Jim was 3 years old on his last birthday and will be 5 years old on his next birthday. How can that be?
Today is his 4th birthday.

What never asks questions but gets a lot of
    answers?
a doorbell.

^^^^^^^^^^^^^^^^^^^^^^^^^^^^^^^^^^^^

What word contains three 'e's' but only one
    letter?
"Envelope."

^^^^^^^^

What always
    seems to be
    behind time?
a clock face.

^^^^^^^^

Why are mush-
    rooms shaped
    like umbrellas?
Because they grow in damp places.

What is cut and spread out on the table but never eaten?
A deck of cards.

∧∧∧∧∧∧∧∧∧∧∧∧∧∧∧∧∧∧∧∧∧∧∧∧∧∧∧∧∧∧∧

How do seven cousins divide five potatoes?
Mash them.

∧∧∧∧∧∧∧∧∧∧∧∧∧∧∧∧∧∧∧∧∧∧∧∧∧∧∧∧∧∧∧

What word in the English language is usually pronounced wrong even by scholars?
"Wrong."

∧∧∧∧∧∧∧∧∧∧∧∧∧∧∧∧∧∧∧∧∧∧∧∧∧∧∧∧∧∧∧

Teacher: "If the plural of man is men, and the plural of woman is women, what is the plural of child?"
Student: "Twins."

Denise: "I know a man who shaves a dozen
       times a day."
Lindy: "Who in the world is that?"
Denise: "The barber."

^^^^^^^^^^^^^^^^^^^^^^^^^^^^^^^^

What button will you never lose?
Your belly button.

^^^^^^^^^^^

What's the best relief
    for ingrown toe-
    nails?
Ingrown toes.

^^^^^^^^^^^

Why do skeletons
    stay home
    every night?
They have no body to go out with.

145

Why are ice cubes kept in the freezer?
To keep the freezer cold.

^^^^^^^^^^^^^^^^^^^^^^^^^^^^^^^

What's long, sharp and one-eyed?
a needle.

^^^^^^^^^^^^^^^^^^^^^^^^^^^^^^^

Why were the ten toes nervous?
They were being followed by two heels.

^^^^^^^^^^^^^^^^^^^^^^^^^^^^^^^

What's the tiniest room you'll ever find?
a mushroom.

^^^^^^^^^^^^^^^^^^^^^^^^^^^^^^^

Which month has 28 days?
all 12 of them.

What vegetable is a plumber's best friend?
a leek.

^^^^^^^^^^^^^^^^^^^^^^^^^^^^^^^^

What gets larger if you take anything away
  from it?
a hole.

^^^^^^^^^^^^^^^^^^^^^^^^^^^^^^^^

What has a fork and a
  mouth, but never
  eats food?
a river.

^^^^^^^

How is an
  apple like a
  pair of roller
  skates?
Both have caused the fall of humans.

What did one math teacher say to the
other?
I've got a problem.

^^^^^^^^^^^^^^^^^^^^^^^^^^^^^^^

Before the discovery of Australia, what was
the earth's largest island?
Australia.

^^^^^^^^^^^^^^^^^^^^^^^^^^^^^^^

What's the noblest item ever made from a
piece of wood?
A ruler.

SCHOOL

Geography Teacher:
"Copley, can you tell me
where Amsterdam is?"
Copley: "Er—here it is!
Page 75!"

^^^^^^^^^^^^^^^^^^^^^^^^^^^^^^^^^^^^^

Where do numbers take a bath?
In mathtubs.

^^^^^^^^^^^^^^^^^^^^^^^^^^^^^^^^^

Teacher: "What are zebras good for?"
Student: "To illustrate the letter 'z.'"

149

Literature Teacher: "Otto, can you tell us who Homer was?"
Otto: "He was Mickey Mantle's sidekick."

∧∧∧∧∧∧∧∧∧∧∧∧∧∧∧∧∧∧∧∧∧∧∧∧∧∧∧∧∧

Teacher: "Do you think it was just as easy to explore the Arctic as it was Antarctica?"
Student: "I don't know. . . .There's a world of difference."

∧∧∧∧∧∧∧∧∧∧∧∧∧∧∧∧∧∧∧∧∧∧∧∧∧∧∧∧∧

Teacher: "How can one child make so many mistakes in one day?"
Student: "By getting up early."

∧∧∧∧∧∧∧∧∧∧∧∧∧∧∧∧∧∧∧∧∧∧∧∧∧∧∧∧∧

Teacher: "Everyone write down the number 11."
Student: "Which 1 comes first?"

A little boy walked up to the teacher's desk and said, "Miss Phillips, I've got bad news for you."

"What is it?" asked Miss Phillips.

"I'm afraid you're in big trouble."

"And why is that?"

"Well, my father says if my grades don't pick up, somebody's in for a beating."

^^^^^^^^^^^^^^^^^^^^^^^^^^^^^^

What's the capital of Wyoming?
That's easy:
"W."

^^^^^^

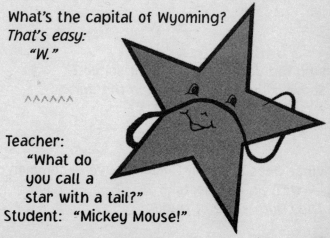

Teacher: "What do you call a star with a tail?"
Student: "Mickey Mouse!"

Marcie: "How do you spell 'inneapolis?' "
Slater: "Don't you mean 'Minneapolis?' "
Marcie: "No, I've already got the 'M.' "

∧∧∧∧∧∧∧∧∧∧∧∧∧∧∧∧∧∧∧∧∧∧∧∧∧∧∧∧∧

Andy: "The teacher sure kept me busy
    today."
Michelle: "What was your assignment?"
Andy: "She put me in a round room and
    told me to sit in the corner."

∧∧∧∧∧∧∧∧∧∧∧∧∧∧∧∧∧∧∧∧∧∧∧∧∧∧∧∧∧

Why did Jerome go to night school?
So he could learn to read in the dark.

∧∧∧∧∧∧∧∧∧∧∧∧∧∧∧∧∧∧∧∧∧∧∧∧∧∧∧∧∧

What does a school teacher have in common
    with an eye doctor?
They both stare at pupils.

Teacher: "Have you ever read much Shakespeare before now?"
New Student: "I don't think so. Who wrote it?"

^^^^^^^^^^^^^^^^^^^^^^^

Teacher: "You didn't answer the last two questions on the test."
Student: "Oh. Well, the answers are stuck inside my fountain pen."

^^^^^^^^^^^^^^^^^^^^^^^

Lila arrived for her second day of first grade carrying a ladder.

"What's the ladder for?" asked a friend.

"I'm ready for high school," Lila said.

What's more difficult than cutting school?
Taping it back together.

∧∧∧∧∧∧∧∧∧∧∧∧∧∧∧∧∧∧∧∧∧∧∧∧∧∧∧∧∧

Ken: "What are you looking for?"

Kelley: "My earring."

Ken: "I'll help. Where do you think you lost it?"

Kelley: "Down in the science lab."

Ken: "Then why in the world are we looking for it here in the lunchroom?"

Kelley: "The light's much brighter in here."

∧∧∧∧∧∧∧∧∧∧∧∧∧∧∧∧∧∧∧∧∧∧∧∧∧∧∧∧∧∧

Teacher: "Why haven't you turned in your homework?"

Student: "I accidentally used the paper to make a paper airplane."

Teacher: "Where's the airplane?"

Student: "Somebody skyjacked it."

Teacher: "Jory, what do you think of Shakespeare's writings?"

Jory: "I think much of what he wrote was a dreadful tragedy."

^^^^^^^^^^^^^^^^^^^^^^^^^^^^^^^^^^^^^^^

Did you hear about the school teacher who was so suspicious while giving tests that his eyes watched each other?

^^^^^^^

Perry: "Your lunch box has a glass top. That's neat!"

Tammy: "Yes. When I'm on the bus, I can easily tell whether I'm going to school or going home."

Teacher: "Warren, can you spell
    Mississippi?"
Warren: "Do you want me to spell the state
    or the river?"

∧∧∧∧∧∧∧∧∧∧∧∧∧∧∧∧∧∧∧∧∧∧∧∧∧∧∧∧∧

First-Grade Teacher: "Hubie, what comes
    after 'g?' "
Hubie: "Whiz."

∧∧∧∧∧∧∧∧∧∧∧∧∧∧∧∧∧∧∧∧∧∧∧∧∧∧∧∧∧

Teacher: "You missed school yesterday,
    didn't you?"
Arnold: "No, not much."

∧∧∧∧∧∧∧∧∧∧∧∧∧∧∧∧∧∧∧∧∧∧∧∧∧∧∧∧∧

Teacher: "Are you having trouble with the
    test questions?"
Student: "Just with the answers."

Wally: "I heard you had to stay in at recess. Did the teacher make you write the same sentence over and over?"

Henry: "No. She kept me busy, though."

Wally: "Doing what?"

Henry: "She gave me a piece of paper that said 'See other side.'"

Wally: "So what did it say on the other side?"

Henry: "That side said 'See other side,' too."

^^^^^^^

A student drew a picture of a stage coach with no wheels.

"What holds it up?" asked the teacher.

"Outlaws."

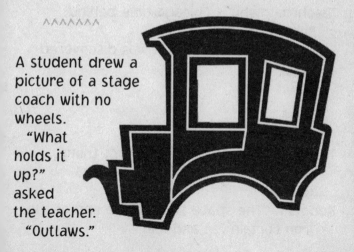

Mother: "What did you learn in school today?"

Elena: "We learned to say 'Yes, Ma'am' and 'Yes, Sir.' "

Mother: "That's wonderful! You'll remember it, won't you?"

Elena: "Yeah, I guess."

∧∧∧∧∧∧∧∧∧∧∧∧∧∧∧∧∧∧∧∧∧∧∧∧∧∧∧∧∧∧

Teacher: "Why is Chicago time behind Boston time?"

Student: "Because Boston was discovered first."

∧∧∧∧∧∧∧∧∧∧∧∧∧∧∧∧∧∧∧∧∧∧∧∧∧∧∧∧∧∧

Teacher: "Name three important things that have occurred in the past 25 years."

Rodger: "The space shuttle, the end of the Iron Curtain . . . and me!"

Teacher: "How many seconds in a minute?"

Don: "Sixty."

Teacher: "That's right. So how many seconds in an hour."

Don, after a long calculation: "Three-thousand, six-hundred."

Teacher: "Very good! Now, this is a hard one: How many seconds in a year?"

Don: "Twelve."

Teacher: "Twelve? How do you get that?"

Don: "January 2nd, February 2nd, March 2nd. . ."

^^^^^^^^^^^^^^^^^^^

"Teacher, I just swallowed my fountain pen!" George screamed.

"Then you may finish the test with your pencil."

What's the favorite drink of cheerleaders?
Root beer.

∧∧∧∧∧∧∧∧∧∧∧∧∧∧∧∧∧∧∧∧∧∧∧∧∧∧∧∧

Teacher: "Kenny, compose a sentence using the word 'archaic.' "
Kenny: "We all know we can't have archaic and eat it, too."

∧∧∧∧∧∧∧∧∧∧∧∧∧∧∧∧∧∧∧∧∧∧∧∧∧∧∧∧

When do leaves start to turn?
The night before a big test.

∧∧∧∧∧∧∧∧∧∧∧∧∧∧∧∧∧∧∧∧∧∧∧∧∧∧∧∧

The teacher asked Marie, "Please go to the map and locate Cuba."

Marie quickly found Cuba on the map at the front of the room.

"That's good, Marie. Now class, can anyone tell me who discovered Cuba?"

Derek quickly raised his hand. "Marie!"

Teacher: "In the Old West, what was cow-
    hide mainly used for?"
Student: "To keep the cow in one piece?"

^^^^^^^^^^^^^^^^^^^^^^^^^^^^^^^

Teacher: "Are you chewing gum?"
New Student: "No, I'm Alison."

^^^^^^^^^^^^^^^^^^^^^^^^^^^^^^^

Teacher: "If you found a
    dollar in your left
    trousers
    pocket and
    65 cents in
    your right
    pocket, what
    would you
    have?"
Student:
    "Somebody
    else's britches."

When little Josie came home from her first day at school, her mother asked, "So how do you like school, Josie?"

"Closed," Josie said.

∧∧∧∧∧∧∧∧∧∧∧∧∧∧∧∧∧∧∧∧∧∧∧∧∧∧∧

Virgil: "How do you spell 'telephone?'"
Shana: "T-e-l-e-p-h-o-n-e. If you would read the dictionary, you would know that yourself."
Virgil: "Hmm. I don't think I want to read the dictionary. I'll wait for the movie."

∧∧∧∧∧∧∧∧∧∧∧∧∧∧∧∧∧∧∧∧∧∧∧∧∧∧∧

Nina came home from school and told her mother, "Our teachers talk to themselves too much."

"Really? Do you think they realize it?"

"Nah. They think students are listening to them."

Teacher: "Robert, how do you spell 'ele-vate?'"

Robert: "E-l-a-v-a-t."

Teacher: "No, that's not the way it's spelled in the dictionary."

Robert: "You asked me how I spelled it, not the dictionary."

SCIENCE

Meg: "Did you know there are more than a thousand miles of blood vessels in the human body?"

Peg: "Really? No wonder my dad complains of tired blood."

^^^^^^^^^^^^^^^^^^^^^^^^^^^^^^^^

"How did the new satellite pictures of California turn out?" one NASA scientist asked another.

"Not so good," said the other. "Someone moved."

Teacher: "What's the difference between air and water?"

Student: "Air can get wetter. Water can't."

^^^^^^^^^^^^^^^^^^^^^^^^^^^^^^^^^^

Teacher: "Who was the first brother to fly an airplane at Kitty Hawk, NC? Was it Orville or Wilbur?"

"Orville!" shouted one student.

"Wilbur!" shouted another.

"They're both Wright," said a third.

^^^^^

Where do stars and planets go to school?

At the universe-ity.

Why were the Wright Brothers first in flight?
Because they weren't wrong.

^^^^^^^^^^^^^^^^^^^^^^^^^^^^^^^^^^^^^

"I didn't understand the science teacher's lesson about the sky today," said Jan.
"Why not?" asked her father.
"It was way over my head."

^^^^^^^^^^^^^^^^^^^^^^^^^^^^^^^^^^^^^

What do you call 4-day-old pizza?
a science project.

SLEEP

"I can't go to sleep at night," complained Ardie.

"Have you tried counting sheep?" asked Mardie.

"How will that help?"

"It'll bore you, and you'll fall asleep."

A few days later, Mardie asked, "Have you been able to sleep?"

"Nope," said Ardie.

"Did you try counting sheep?"

"Yep. I got up to 3,628."

"Then what happened?"

"Well, then it was time to get up."

"What are you doing in front of the mirror with your eyes closed?"
"I've always wondered what I look like when I'm asleep."

∧∧∧∧∧∧∧∧∧∧∧∧∧∧∧∧∧∧∧∧∧∧∧∧∧∧∧∧∧∧∧∧

What happens if you sleep with a bar of soap under your pillow?
You'll slip out of bed in the morning.

SPORTS

Hoyt: "I think sports are boring."

Bonnie: "Why do you think so?"

Hoyt: "I can always tell you the score before the game even begins."

Bonnie: "Really?"

Hoyt: "Sure. It's 0 to 0."

^^^^^^^^^^^^^^^^^^^^^^^^^^^^^^^^^^^^

What do four balls mean in baseball?
They mean you can lose three and still be okay.

Why do golfers carry extra socks?
In case they get a hole in one.

∧∧∧∧∧∧∧∧∧∧∧∧∧∧∧∧∧∧∧∧∧∧∧∧∧∧∧∧∧

Harry: "Who was the first golfer in history?"
Sherry: "I don't know. Sam Snead?"
Harry: "No—Magellan. He went around in
    1519."

∧∧∧∧∧∧∧∧∧∧∧∧∧∧∧∧∧∧∧∧∧∧∧∧∧∧∧∧∧

What did the SCUBA diver find quaking at
    the bottom of the bay?
A nervous wreck.

∧∧∧∧∧∧∧∧∧∧∧∧∧∧∧∧∧∧∧∧∧∧∧∧∧∧∧∧∧

Coach: "So you think you know everything
    there is to know about soccer?"
New Player: "I do."
Coach: "Then how many holes are in the
    goal net?"

"You'll never make the basketball team," said Herman. "You're too short."

"But maybe," said Hank, "I could lie about my height."

^^^^^^^^^^^^^^^^^^^^^^^^^^^^^^^^^^^^^^

Reporter: "Why are you a skydiver? Isn't it extremely dangerous jumping out of airplanes?"

Skydiver: "No, jumping is a piece of cake—but it does get risky as you approach the ground."

^^^^^^^^^^^^^^^^^^^^^^^^

Why do hockey players spend all their time on ice?
Because their skates would bog down in the sand.

STATES

"What's your name?"
"Tex."
"You're from Texas?"
"Nope, Connecticut. I don't like being called 'Con.'"

^^^^^^^^^^^^^^^^^^^^^^^^^^^^^^^^^^

Rachel: "Did you know the USA has four new states?"

Shelby: "You mean, besides Hawaii and Alaska?"

Rachel: "Yes—New Hampshire, New Jersey, New Mexico and New York."

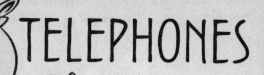

TELEPHONES

"This phone cord's too long," a woman said. "I'm always tripping over it. See what you can do to fix it."

So her husband called the phone company. "Our phone cord's too long," he said. "Pull in about five feet of slack, please."

^^^^^^^^^^^^^^^^^^^^^^^^^^^^^^^^

Why didn't Josie pay her telephone bill?
She believed in free speech.

What happens when you dial 116?
*The ambulance rushes to your house upside
  down.*

∧∧∧∧∧∧∧∧∧∧∧∧∧∧∧∧∧∧∧∧∧∧∧∧∧∧∧∧∧∧∧

"Charity, please answer the phone for me!"
Mother told Charity.
  "Sure," Charity said, running to grab the
receiver. "Hello, phone."

∧∧∧∧∧∧∧∧∧∧∧∧∧∧∧∧∧∧∧∧∧∧∧∧∧∧∧∧∧∧∧

"Did you know that certain people who are
almost deaf can still use the telephone?"
Erin asked.
  "No," replied Joey, "but a lot of dumb people certainly use it."

TELEVISION & RADIO

"Are you going to watch the eclipse of the moon tonight?"

"Depends on which channel. We don't get cable TV."

^^^^^^^^^^^^^^^^^^^^^^^^^^^^^^^^^^^^^^^

"My sister doesn't like our new computer."
   "Why not?"
   "It doesn't get The Disney Channel."

175

Why did Albert put his radio in the freezer?
He wanted to hear some cool music.

^^^^^^^^^^^^^^^^^^^^^^^^^^^^^^^

Art: "Did you hear the concert on the radio
last night?"
Keri: "My radio won't come on at night."
Art: "What's wrong with it?"
Keri: "It's an AM radio."

^^^^^^^^^^^^^^^^^^^^^^^^^^^^^^^

Blair: "Sometimes I wonder about Kippie."
Dirk: "Why is that?"
Blair: "He tried to find the English Channel
on cable TV."

VACATIONS

Henry: "Mom, why are we packing soap in the suitcase?"

Mom: "We'll need it for the trip."

Henry: "But I thought this was supposed to be a vacation."

^^^^^^^^^^^^^^^^^^^^^^^^^^^^^^^^^^

Brad: "I can get from Philadelphia to Baltimore without buying a ticket."

Joanna: "How?"

Brad: "Walk."

Nickie: "I've finally saved up enough money to go to Hawaii!"

Mickie: "Great! When are you going?"

Nickie: "As soon as I save up enough to get back."

∧∧∧∧∧∧∧∧∧∧∧∧∧∧∧∧∧∧∧∧∧∧∧∧∧∧∧

A troop of girl scouts were huddling around a campfire. "Can bears see at night?" Cindy asked nervously.

"I reckon they have to," Wren suggested. "They aren't able to hold flashlights."

∧∧∧∧∧∧∧∧∧∧∧∧∧∧∧∧∧∧∧∧∧∧∧∧∧∧∧

Randy and Andy visited the beach for the first time in their lives. "Wow! Look at all the water!" Randy shouted.

"Yeah—and that's only the surface!" Andy said.

Father: "Jack, why did you put a beetle in your sister's sleeping bag?"

Jack: "I couldn't find a snake."

^^^^^^^^^^^^^^^^^^^^^^^^^^^^^^^^^^^^

Trail Guide: "You don't have to worry about riding along those narrow mountain trails. These donkeys are sure-footed critters."

Tourist: "Does that mean when they kick, they don't miss?"

WHAT'S THAT?

What's black and shriveled up and giggles?

a ticklish raisin.

^^^^^^^^^^^^^^^^^^^^^^^^^^^^^^^

What do you get when you cross a praying mantis with a termite?

an insect that returns thanks before eating your floors.

What do you call two bars of soap?
a pair of slippers.

^^^^^^^^^^^^^^^^^^^^^^^^^^^^^^

What's blue and red and headed for the
    doctor's office?
a tomato with frostbite.

^^^^^^^^^

What says, "Tick-
    tock-ruff-
    ruff?"
a watchdog.

^^^^^^^^^^^^^^^^

What do you get when you
    cross a camel with a
    station wagon?
a camel that seats nine.

What's long and green and very dangerous?
a herd of charging cucumbers.

^^^^^^^^^^^^^^^^^^^^^^^^^^^^^^^^^^^^^

What's purple and wears a mask?
The Lone Grape.

^^^^^^^^^^^^^^^^^^^^^^^^^^^^^^^^^^

What has one head and four legs?
a bed.

^^^^^^^^^^^^^^^^^^^^^^^^^^^^^^^^^^^^

What's long and slimy, swims, carries a sub-
machine gun and honks a horn?
a auto-mob-eel.

^^^^^^^^^^^^^^^^^^^^^^^^^^^^^^^^^^

What's the opposite of minimum?
Minipop.

What do you get when you cross a woodpecker and a carrier pigeon?
*A bird that knocks before delivering the
message.*

∧∧∧∧∧∧∧∧∧∧∧∧∧∧∧∧∧∧∧∧∧∧∧∧∧∧∧∧∧∧∧∧

What's long and yellow and helps elderly
ladies across the street?
Banana Scouts.

∧∧∧∧∧∧∧∧∧∧

What do you get
when you cross
a parrot with a
grizzly bear?
 Whatever it
is, if it says,
"Polly wanna
cracker," you
better give it a
whole box!

What's yellow, has four doors and lies on its
    back?
A sick taxicab.

^^^^^^^^^^^^^^^^^^^^^^^^^^^^^^^^^^^

What do you get when you cross a rooster
    and a bull?
Roost beef.

^^^^^^^^^^^^^^^^^^^^^^^^^^^^^^^^^^^

What has three heads, two arms, two wings,
    eight legs and two tails?
A horseback rider carrying a falcon.

^^^^^^^^^^^^^^^^^^^^^^^^^^^^^^^^^^^

What animal sees just as well from one end
    as the other?
A blind one.

What's purple and goes, "Slam! Slam!"
A two-door grape.

^^^^^^^^^^^^^^^^^^^^^^^^^^^^^^^^^^^^^

What's hairy and sneezes?
A peach with a cold.

^^^^^^^^^^^^^^^^^^^^^^^^^^^^^^^^^^^^^

What hops around holding up banks?
A robbit.

^^^^^^

What do you
   call a
   young fox
   after it's 30
   days old?
Thirty-one days old.

WORK

"Did you hear Harry went to work at the bank?"

"No. Why does he want to work at a bank?"

"He heard there's money in it."

^^^^^^^^^^^^^^^^^^^^^^^^^^^^^^^^

Boss: "You drive nails like lightning."

Carpenter: "Pretty fast, huh?"

Boss: "Nope—you never hammer the same place twice."

Why did the weather announcer quit her job?
She didn't find the weather very agreeable.

^^^^^^^^^^^^^^^^^^^^^^^^^^^^^^^

Will: "I just heard they aren't building rail-road tracks any longer."
Sam: "Why not?"
Will: "They're already long enough."

^^^^^^^^^^^^

Molly: "Why did your father go to work at the bakery?"
Allie: "He kneads the dough."

ODDS & ENDS

Why did Miriam put a bag of ice under her aunt's easy chair?

She wanted to see Auntie freeze.

∧∧∧∧∧∧∧∧∧∧∧∧∧∧∧∧∧∧∧∧∧∧∧∧∧∧∧

Two walls were talking to each other when a man overheard them and shouted, "Be quiet!"

"Come on," one wall whispered softly to the other. "I'll meet you at the corner and we can finish our discussion."

Why won't a bicycle stand up when it's not
   moving?
It's two-tired.

^^^^^^^^^^^^^^^

Why did Lindy carry
   her umbrella
   to school?
*She didn't want to leave
   it home alone.*

^^^^^^^^^^^^^

Morris: "Did you
   hear about the
   skeleton who
   became a movie
   star?"
Glenda: "How did he
   do that?"
Morris: "He had good
   connections."

Mother: "Has Clay finished changing that light bulb yet?"

Billy: "I don't think so. He keeps breaking them accidentally with the hammer."

∧∧∧∧∧∧∧∧∧∧∧∧∧∧∧∧∧∧∧∧∧∧∧∧∧∧∧∧

Carey: "You sure have a weird name."

Bretopnius: "It's better than the one my father first pulled out of the hat."

Carey: "What was that?"

Bretopnius: "Eight-and-a-Quarter."

∧∧∧∧∧∧∧∧∧∧∧∧∧∧∧∧∧∧∧∧∧∧∧∧∧∧∧∧

Jamie's kitten had climbed high up a tree, and she said it wouldn't come down, no matter how long she coaxed. "What can we do?" she asked her father.

"Wait until September. He'll catch the first leaf that falls and float right to the ground."

What cowboy wears a black mask just like the Lone Ranger's, rides a horse just like Silver and has a sidekick who could be Tonto's twin brother?
The Clone Ranger.

^^^^^^^^^^^^^^^^^^^^^^^^^^^^^^^^^^

Winona: "Did you hear the McMillans are moving to Gettysburg?"

Andrea: "No. Why are they moving?"

Winona: "Because they want to have a Gettysburg address."

^^^^^^^^^^^^

How did the cat succeed in winning a starring role in a movie?
With purr-sistence.

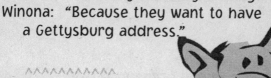

Fran: "Why does your family have a mirror on the bathroom ceiling?"

Dan: "So we can see ourselves gargle."

∧∧∧∧∧∧∧∧∧∧∧∧∧∧∧∧∧∧∧∧∧∧∧∧∧∧∧∧

Mother: "You're not being selfish with the sled, are you Jenny? You're letting your little sister use it half the time?"

Jenny: "Yes, Ma'am. I use it coming down the hill and she uses it going up."

∧∧∧∧∧∧∧∧∧∧∧∧∧∧∧∧∧∧∧∧∧∧∧∧∧∧∧∧

Gavin: "How do you pronounce t-o?"

Grady: "To."

Gavin: "What about t-w-o?"

Grady: "Two."

Gavin: "And how do you pronounce the second day of the week?"

Grady: "Tuesday."

Gavin: "Wrong. It's Monday."